THE HAPPY BREWER

—the principles and practice of home brewing

Dedication

To a very courageous little lady

— my Ruth

The

Happy Brewer

—the principles and practice of home brewing

by

W. G. NEWSOM

© "The Amateur Winemaker" Publications Ltd. 1978

ISBN 0 900841 49 4

1st EDITION

First Impression—March 1978

Printed in Great Britain by
Standard Press (Andover) Ltd., South Street, Andover, Hants.

Contents

Chapter		*Page*
	Preface	9
I	The History of Beer	11
II	How to Brew	18
III	Water	24
IV	Hops	30
V	Malting and Milling	39
VI	Yeast	45
VII	Sugars, Carbohydrates and Albuminoids	52
VIII	Mashing and Sparging	57
IX	Boiling and Cooling	65
X	The Use of the Hydrometer	67
XI	Fermentation	72
XII	Draught Beer Production	75
XIII	Fining and Filtration	81
XIV	Beer Types, Draught and Bottled	85
XV	Conditioning Beer	92
XVI	Basic Recipes	95
XVII	Judging Beers	102
XVIII	Cooking with Beer	106

Contents

Chapter   Page

I   The History of Beer   11
II   How to Brew
III   Water
IV   Hops
V   Malting and Milling
VI
VII
VIII   Yeast and Yeasting
IX   Racking and Fining
X   Control of the Hydrometer
XI   Fermentation
XII
XIII
XIV
XV   Colour Control
XVI
XVII
XVIII

Preface

Here at last is a book that successfully bridges the gap between the amateur and professional brewer. Written in an authoritative and informative style by a dedicated craftsman-brewer whose wealth of practical experience and theoretical knowledge has rightly merited him the esteem and respect of fellow brewers in both the amateur and professional fields.

With family interests in the trade when beer was beer and cellarcraft was more than just pressurising kegs, Wilf Newsom learnt basic fundamentals and gained invaluable experience which has held him in good stead ever since. Following the revival of amateur wine and beer making since the war, Wilf has been in the forefront in raising the standard of home-brew and as a founder member of the Amateur National Guild of Judges, he laid down the rules for judging beer and method of examination for potential beer judges. I find the book unique in its presentation of the subject, being a partnership of sound traditional craft practices strengthened—not displaced by—scientific principles and current brewing technology.

The novice is taken by the hand and guided along the elementary road of simple basic recipes and methods. Having whetted his appetite, the author then leads him on to more advanced techniques, and opens the door into the true world of brewing.

This is certainly a book that will stimulate the reader to develop his own potential in the fascinating and rewarding hobby of brewing.

Don Hebbs.

CHAPTER I

THE HISTORY OF BEER

The brewing of beer is as old as history.

Mythology has it that the gods showed man how to brew beer to compensate him for the troubles he has to endure. Herodotus credited the invention of brewing to Bacchus, the Egyptians claimed the honour for Isis or Osiris, and the Germans for a legendary king, Gambrinus. You can take your pick, for it isn't really important who it was. What is important is that brewing once an art, has in subsequent centuries transformed itself into a science. It is remarkable, though, that it was not until the middle of the nineteenth century that beer came under the microscope, the microscope being that of none other than that great man, Louis Pasteur. His publication "Études sur la Bière" paved the way for the now accepted scientific approach to brewing. He, Emil Chris Hansen and Alfred Jorgensen, possibly did more than anyone else for the advancement of brewing. It was Hansen who discovered how to isolate and develop pure culture yeast and naturally he wished to patent his apparatus, but J. C. Jacobsen the brewer of the Carlsberg brewery would not hear of this, saying that the Carlsberg brewery would publish the results of research for anyone who wished to read them. It would perhaps be a happy gesture, to allocate Jacobsen a niche in our hall of fame as well.

Reference to the brewing of beer in the Tigris and Euphrates was made in the Book of the Dead some 4,000 years B.C. The Egyptians used to make a "barley cake" which, after baking, was crushed, placed in hot water and fermented. This form of beer was called "Boozah", a word which has a familiar sound, if not the same spelling, today!

Beer slaked the thirst of the Pharaohs, and many a Roman Legionnaire and Centurion must have been grateful for its revivifying qualities after battle. In the Middle Ages continual wars in Europe ravaged the vineyards and beer became the main beverage of the soldiery, and even in the 1939–45 conflict beer was still sometimes given high priority. When British troops entered Milan, part of the spoils captured was a trainload of malt and general brewing materials despatched from Germany for their troops on the Italian front. A senior British officer called for anyone with brewing experience and got no less than a complete brewery staff! Production got under way in a mineral water factory and a very creditable brew was placed before the beer-starved troops!

Throughout history the church has always been to the fore in the making of wines and beers, and modern brewing owes much to the foundations they laid. The monk Groll, for instance, was really responsible for the fame of the Pilsen lager, and many of the beers we enjoy today have their origin in brews made by the church.

Special occasions produced special brews. In the Middle Ages, for example, education was increasing and the church found that its colleges were getting an ever-increasing amount of pupils. Larger colleges and more pupils meant more finances. More finances involved balance sheets, and balance sheets in turn involved auditors. The important visit by the auditors once a year was the signal for a specially strong beer to be brewed, and this became known as Audit ale.

One would like to be generous and say that they were made as a gesture of courtesy to the auditors. Tasting these ales and realising their strength, however, one begins to be a little suspicious, and cannot help wondering if the brewers did not perhaps have ulterior motives. These beers—rather expensive —can still be bought today at the main University towns and Colleges, such as New College Oxford. What better place to try a glass with history all around one!

In Britain, doubtless because an unpredictable climate did not favour winegrowing, ale became the nation's natural drink, and over the centuries we have amassed such expertise and know-how that, together with Germany, we must be considered the world's leading brewers.

The ancient Britons made mead, and there is a strong probability that they also brewed a form of beer and used honey to put extra body and strength into it. Primarily however, it was the women in Britain who made the beer and they were known as "Ale Wives", or brewsters (a female brewer). Hence our words "Brewster Sessions". They were in fact brewer, public house and inn keeper, cook, and washerwoman and would outclass Figaro as a general factotum. In the

Middle Ages Billingsgate was already established as London's fish market and the water used for cleaning the fish came downstream and was eventually used by a great number of ale wives who used to congregate at that particular spot. Beer was even then known as "Wallop", and one wonders whether this could be whence the term "Cod's Wallop"—meaning trash—came in! Certainly hygiene was not very high on their list of priorities!

Britain is unique in the field of brewing in that nearly all its inns and public-houses display a sign outside which tells the traveller pictorially its name. We have names like "The Oak", "The World Upside Down", "The Fox", "The Plough", "The Swan With Two Necks", "The Three Horseshoes", and so on. Most of these signs and titles have historical significance and doubtless originated in the days when very few could read or write, but a sign or picture would convey to the illiterate the type of service being given. At the very beginning there were no such exotic signs. All the ale wife used to tell the public that she brewed ale was a long pole, usually over the door, and looking like a flag pole. If her beer was ready for serving she would tie a bush of hops to the pole and the weary and thirsty raveller on seeing this would enter and take his fill. In London today we have a reminder of those days for in the district that was the grazing ground for flocks of sheep, the shepherds used one favourite ale house when its bush of hops was begin displayed. That district is Shepherds Bush, now no longer, alas, an idyllic scene of quiet, green fields, and grazing sheep, but a concrete jungle of television studios, roaring traffic and Diesel fumes.

One of the first records of beer being brewed is at Burton Abbey in 1295, but many years were to elapse before brewing received official recognition; that in fact came in 1437, when Henry VI gave the Brewers Company its Charter.

Whilst hops are known to have been used for brewing some time before the early sixteenth century that is the period which is usually credited with their large-scale introduction into Britain. This was probably due to the influence of the Dutch who liked a bitter beer, as opposed to the hopless ale until then popular in Britain.

In the reign of Queen Elizabeth I beer seems to have been

the staple beverage of the day. The queen's maids of honour were given a personal issue of two gallons of a beer called "Doble-Doble"—FOR BREAKFAST! One wonders whether this issue was made by the preceding monarch, Henry VIII. If so it would explain the merriment of the Wives of Windsor and their pursuit of the rotund Falstaff through Windsor Great Park!

Since most of the pleasurable things in life eventually attract the eagle eye of the tax-collector it is not to be wondered at that sooner or later beer would do likewise, and it was King Charles I who gave his assent to beer being taxed for the first time. It was Charles II however, who appears to have been the tutor to succeeding Chancellors of Exchequers, for he decreed a tax of 3d per barrel on strong beer and $\frac{1}{3}$d. per barrel on the weaker stuff. Not content with that, malt was taxed in 1697 and sometimes afterwards hops suffered the same fate.

Inns and ale houses have always had their place in history. Many inns between London and York lay claim to having housed one or more of the many highwaymen who haunted this famous route. But the romanticism and glamour now commonly associated with these gentlemen is very much the imaginative creation of later writers. In fact they were usually a cowardly, arrogant, merciless lot, who used the inns at will, exacting secrecy and silence from the unfortunate inn-keepers by threats. Some landlords, less scrupulous, used their inns as clearing houses for stolen goods, a profitable sideline. It does not need a great deal of imagination to picture the many deals, hagglings, and efforts to cheat, with a loaded pistol or blunderbuss nearby to act as the final judge, and all this over a "friendly" (?) jar of ale. Abroad, the vast, new, exciting continent of America was attracting people, eager to begin a new way of life, Religious dissidents like the Pilgrim Fathers were leaving this country, and were being joined by French, German, Italian and Russian settlers; all the countries of Europe were sending emigrants. As these grew in numbers and the initial pioneering was completed, towns began to spring up and with them the general desire to return to some of their former ways of life, including the enjoyment of a tankard of beer, ale, lager, or porter. Brewers started to arrive from Europe and before long breweries were in full swing. The

Germans and others used the decoction system, the British settlers the traditional infusion system of brewing. It is interesting to note that today those two systems are still in use, but some breweries have adopted a compromise.

Brewing up to the beginning of the 19th century was very much a hit and miss affair, and many breweries would not brew in the hot, summer months as their beers went "off". At that time little was known of hygiene, and even less about micro-organisms and bacterial infections. Although Leeuwenhoek developed the microscope in the 17th century it was not until the latter half of the 19th century that it was used for brewing purposes. Little was known of fermentation, and in the early 1800's Levesques wrote in his book "The Art of Brewing and Fermenting": "Fermentation is a slow motion of the intestine particles of a mixed body, arising usually from the operation of some active acid matter which rarifies, exalts, and subtilises the soft sulflureous particles as when leven or yeast lightens and ferments bread or wort".

The real breakthrough came in 1857 when Louis Pasteur published the results of his research. These included many analyses, culture techniques and the principles of sterilisation. This research benefited posterity in many ways, and today, for instance, Pasteurisation is a household word. Although Pasteur's work was recognised—for he came to England and did research in one or two breweries—it did not make an immediate impact on the brewing industry, but his work did pave the way for E. C. Hansen who was to follow him. Many of the old principles of brewing were cast aside. Cleanliness, sterilisation, microbiology, and biochemistry became matters for research and close study, and today brewing is a vast science, with untold wealth pouring in and out of its coffers. One wonders what our ancient Egyptian brewer, the old ale wife, or indeed a lady-in-waiting to Elizabeth I would say if they could see this remarkable transformation.

Finally let us look at some names and see what influence they have had on brewing—both for better or worse.

ALLSOPP, of Burton, whose foresight led him to bring in the first scientist to brewing in 1845.

BASS, William, probably as famous as Worthington, started out as a brewery carter in Burton but was convinced that he

15

would be a better brewer. In 1777 he sold his cartage business to Pickfords and started his own brewery. His fame was enhanced when the brewery brought out a great Pale Ale which was exported to India, and shortly after found a deserved fame in this country.

BAVERSTOCK, who discovered the Saccharometer in 1785, thus giving brewing one of the first steps in scientific control.

DALE, Arthur T. The founder of the "Brewers Show" in 1879. Now called the "Brewers Exhibition" and held in London.

FAHRENHEIT, who invented a thermometer scale making the control of brewing more exact. This type of thermometer is being superseded by the Centigrade scale.

GLADSTONE, William, changed the whole system of taxation on beer in 1880. He laid down that a specific sum would be charged for each degree of gravity from the original. This left the brewers with a free hand in preparing the grist, which had formerly been taxed.

GUINNESS, Arthur, once a butler to a bishop, formulated his Extra Stout, left the bishop's service and in 1759 leased the St. James Gate brewery in Dublin for 9,000 years!

GROLL, the Bavarian monk, who, in 1842 was a major factor in the founding of the world famous Pilsen Lager.

HANSEN, Emil Chris, who first isolated a pure yeast cell and in collaboration with Kuhle, the manager of the Carlsberg brewery perfected the apparatus for the continuous production of pure yeast.

HARRISON, James, of Geelong, Victoria, improved the compression machine for refrigeration for practical purposes in 1857. Then Professor Linde of Germany brought out the ammonia compression machine in 1873. These two gentlemen made it possible for the brewing industry to be the first to use artificial refrigeration—a break through in temperature control, so essential to the lager industry.

HENIUS, Dr. Max, co-founder of the Whal-Henius Brewing School in Chicago.

JACOBSEN, J. C., the Danish brewer who realised the significance of the yeast being used in the Spaten brewery in Munich and brought some back to Carlsberg. This yeast, purified, is now the famous sacch. Carlsbergensis.

16

LAMBERT, L., a pioneer in the use of caramels in 1880.

LAUER, Frederick, is credited with being the first to produce lager in Reading, Pennsylvania in 1844. The United States Brewers Association erected a monument to him in 1885, naming him as the father of American brewing.

LEEUWENHOEK, developed the microscope and opened up the field of micro-organisms.

MOORE, Mr., designed the Hop Exchange in Southwark in 1865. Here the growers, factors, and brewers gathered to discuss and purchase their requirements from samples. Alas this grand old building was a victim of the "Blitz" in the last war.

PASTEUR, Louis, one of the greatest scientists to brewing and the world in general. His research brought about the knowledge and study of antibiotics and microbiology.

PETER THE GREAT, CZAR OF RUSSIA, who was studying shipbuilding at Greenwich and Debtford was so impressed with a stout brewed by Barkleys that this very strong beverage was exported to Russia at his request, and became known as Russian Imperial stout.

SCHLITZ, Joseph, owned the first American brewery to use a pure yeast culture which became generally used from about 1800–1890.

WHITBREAD, who was not only a great brewer, but was responsible for the introduction of bottled beer in 1868.

WORTHINGTON, William, one of the worlds' greatest brewers who set up brewing in Burton 1744.

CHAPTER II

HOW TO BREW

There can be nothing more stimulating or satisfying after a hard day's toil, or a game of sport than a glass of beer. What better than a piece of crusty loaf, a knob of butter, a piece of your favourite cheese, and glass or tankard of beer,—particularly if you made the latter? A banquet fit for a king, and nothing better for shaking off that jaded feeling and restoring lost energy. Indeed, a good glass of stout and milk is often recommended to those suffering from anaemia.

Some people shy away from brewing. "Why", they say "should I go to the trouble of making my own beers? Surely it is much easier to stick to buying the commercial products? I suppose I have to buy a lot of equipment which will cost me the earth? And if I buy it, what then? Hours upon hours of messy ingredients, boiling, smells, in fact being a general nuisance to all and sundry. And for what? I suppose the end product will be a pretty filthy looking mess. And if it turns out like this I could not possibly offer it to my friends, so what's the point in starting anyway?"

Fact, or fancy? I can assure you that those points have been put to me many times over the years, and I am delighted to record that many of our now successful brewers break into a broad grin when I remind them that they too once passed such remarks before becoming keen and confirmed beer makers. With this in mind let me answer, quite firmly, some of those points.

Why trouble to make our own beer? Trouble? It is no trouble but a simple task if performed correctly, and the resultant beer has a quality that is hard to surpass.

Easier to buy commercial? Agreed—if you are prepared to pay the high prices for the low gravities. Don't forget, the amateur has no overheads to meet so his beer must be cheaper, and in these days of ever increasing prices this is a salient point indeed. Another important factor is that the individual home brewer can tailor his requirements to suit his own tastes.

18

Expensive equipment? Twaddle, as you will see when you read the paragraph on "Requirements".

Hours spent preparing ingredients etc? Wrong again. Even the most complicated form of brewing can be done neatly and tidily with no inconvenience to anyone. The longest operation, that of mashing grain, does not need constant surveillance, but only an occasional check. On the other hand simple brewing is a fairly quick operation in preparing the wort.

And the taste of the end product? Suffice to say home brewed beers should be, can be, and usually are star bright. Naturally they are bottle matured and will carry a slight sediment, slightly more than their commercial counterpart, but they can be served with a condition and brilliance that are a delight to behold. As for offering it to your friends, here the danger is not in their refusal to drink, but in their delighted acceptance, thus making large inroads into and eventually exhausting your stocks!

To sum up therefore, let us agree that producing beer is an art or a science, or a combination of both. It can be extremely simple or, as in breweries, extremely scientific. This book attempts to cover the salient points of both. There can be no more simple ingredients to use. All that is required is malt (in its many forms), hops (in their many varieties), sugar, yeast, and water. It is the permutations and methods often using these materials that make the differences. But let us not get too complicated at this stage. Let us approach the brewing of beers now in their simplest forms, and then, having mastered that, graduate to the more advanced forms.

I have compiled for you some simple recipes which use easily procured materials, and which give a range of beers comparable with, and in some cases superior to, their commercial counterparts. It must be remembered however, that a little patience is required to acquire the skill which will result in that sparkling, brilliant beer with a head that lasts throughout the glass. So go to it and become one of those much envied people—A BREWER.

Requirements

It is wrong to assume that special equipment is required for simple brewing. The average household utensils lend themselves admirably to use in the preparation and brewing of beer. The main requirement is a large vessel, such as an aluminium or stainless steel preserving pan, if we are to make 5 gallon brews. If one or two gallons is the aim then large saucepans will do. These are for use in heating the ingredients.

Next we need a container in which to carry out the fermentation. A polythene dustbin with a lock-on lid is ideal. These can be obtained from all large departmental stores, wine and beer equipment shops, and hardware stores. If a choice of plastic is available ask for "Dairy Quality"; these will be found easy to keep clean. For a one- or two-gallon brew a plastic two-gallon bucket can be used, again making sure that it is of good quality. Remember at all times to use only rigid plastic. Other materials suitable for fermentation purposes are glass, stainless steel, *salt glazed* pottery, and sound, unchipped enamel containers. Avoid at all costs chipped enamel, zinc, galvanised, and *lead glazed* containers. The golden rule which should be constantly before you should be, "If in doubt—Don't use."

For straining purposes we can use muslin, but white nylon is to be preferred, and for siphoning a 4 ft length of P.V.C., nylon, or rubber tubing of about $\frac{1}{4}''$ bore.

Only genuine beer or cider bottles of the screw-topped or crown-corked variety should be used for bottling. On no account must other bottles be used, for gas pressure created in the "bottle fermentation" will lead to weaker bottles bursting with possible serious results. On no account should the disposable and non-returnable beer bottles be used, for they are made from exceedingly thin glass.

For sterilisation and cleaning purposes use a solution of either Campden tablets or sodium metabisulphite. If 12 Campden tablets are dissolved in a quart of warm water an efficient steriliser is produced. Each tablet contains 7 grains, and knowing this one can make up a solution to suit individual requirements. A more convenient, and cheaper method is to use sodium metabisulphite. Four ounces of this chemical is dissolved in a quart of water to give a 10% stock solution.

Either of these recipes will give a highly anti bacterial solution with a storage life of some months.

If using crown corks as a sealant a crown corking machine will be required. These are fairly easy to obtain, and as many breweries are discontinuing the use of screw stoppers it may be prudent to invest in one of these little machines. They simply hold the crown cork on to the top of the bottle whilst a pair of jaws crimp the edges when you press down two levers. These are vastly superior to the "knock on" type of crown capper.

Preparation

Bring a convenient part of water to be used to the boil. If the container has a lid, so much the better, for it will help to retard the loss of the hop fragrance. Add salt (if called for), then hops and simmer for 45 minutes. Some of the hop fragrance will inevitably be lost, so keep back a few hops out of the weight prescribed and add for the last 5 minutes of the infusion.

Next place the sugar and malt extract into a further amount of the water and heat until completely dissolved; take care to keep stirring. Pour this solution into the fermenting vessel, after which fix a nylon filter or strainer and strain through the hop liquid. The hops should be squeezed dry before discarding. Bring up the volume to the prescribed amount by adding the remainder of the water. You are now ready to commence fermenting. When the temperature is down to 60° F, add the previously activated yeast.

Conducting The Ferment

The time taken between adding the yeast and bottling will vary with the recipe and temperature. For instance, Recipe 1 will take longer to ferment than Recipe 2 because it includes more fermentable sugars. Recipe 1 will take roughly 8–10 days at a temperature of 60° F. It is at this stage that experience will count.

So . . . we have added the yeast and the temperature is 60°–65° F. Twenty four hours after the yeast has been added a heavy foam will be seen. This is skimmed off as it contains some impurities, after which the ferment is allowed to proceed with an occasional skimming to aid the clearing. As the ferment draws to a close, a ring of bubbles will be seen in the centre of the brew, and the top of the beer will be clear—in fact like flat beer! Stand by for bottling.

Bottling

Wash all bottles, stoppers and corks thoroughly. Invert and drain them before adding Campden or Sodium solution. Swill each bottle by pouring from one bottle to the next. If the bottles are sniffed a very strong, pungent odour will be noticed. When the bottles are emptied ignore the odour and fill up with beer; it is not harmful but helpful to the brew. The bottle should be filled with beer to approximately one inch from the base of the stopper. This allows for gas expansion in the bottle and thus minimises the risk of burst bottles. Frightening as this may sound, no trouble will be experienced if these directions are followed. The final bottling process is the priming, when; with the bottles filled to their marks, each quart bottle receives one *level* teaspoon of ordinary white or caster sugar. If you are using pint bottles, put only *half* a teaspoon of sugar in each. The bottles are then firmly screwed down. The sugar starts a small ferment in the bottle thus giving the required sparkle and head. After bottling the beer is left, stored upright, in a cool place for varying amounts of time according to the recipe. Always bear in mind that the heavier the gravity, or the more sugar and malt extract used, the longer the time taken to mature.

Siphoning

To fill your bottles it is advisable to use a siphon, and this operation is quite simple, in fact it is a pleasure! A length of tubing (as previously advised) is inserted into the brew so that the end is about an inch above the sediment. A plastic knitting needle secured with an elastic band so that an inch protrudes beyond the end of the tube will do this. Then suck the liquid through the pipe and when it commences to flow place the end of the tube into the bottle. Make sure that the bottle is well below the level of the bottom of the container, or the beer will flow back. It is a good thing to have a funnel in the bottle with the nylon filter over it so that you filter the beer once more when filling the bottle.

22

RECIPES
Bitter Beer

Recipe 1	*Recipe 2*
5 gallons water	5 gallons water
3 lb. demerara sugar	1½ lb. demerara sugar
1 lb. brown sugar	1 lb. brown sugar
2 lb. malt extract	2½ lb malt extract
5 oz. hops	4 oz. hops
Beer yeast	Beer yeast

Stout

5 gallons water	1 lb. caramelised malt *or*
1½ lb. demerara sugar	½ lb. silcose caramel
1 lb. glucose—chips, powder or syrup	3 oz. hops
2 lb. malt extract	Beer yeast

Brown Ale

5 gallons water	2 lb. bran
1 tablespoon gravy browning	3 lb. demerara sugar
3 oz. hops	Beer yeast

Bring 2–2½ gallons of water to the boil, then add the bran, hops, sugar, and the gravy browning (this is only caramel), and boil gently for 90 minutes. Strain off through nylon filter into fermenting vessel. Top up to 5 gallons, and when cool add yeast and proceed as for other brews. This beer should be ready for bottling after 7–10 days.

Two Lager Types

Light	*Dark (Munich)*
5 gallons water	5 gallons water
11 lb. dried malt extract	12 lb. dried malt extract
5 oz. hops (Lager if available)	4 oz. hops (Lager if available)
Lager yeast	Lager yeast

Boil the malt and hops together for 30 minutes, and when cool add yeast. This should be activated in a "starter bottle" as per instructions supplied with the yeast. Ferment on as usual. The same instructions apply for both recipes. Once the wort becomes activated it is advisable to move it to some cold place to slow down the fermentation. This will mean, of course, that the fermentation will be a lengthy one. Do not be tempted to speed it up. Remember that lager means "stored".

23

CHAPTER III

WATER

Having mastered the basic principles of brewing (and I trust enjoyed the fruits of your labours) you are, I hope, now ready to study more deeply the ingredients from which these many beverages are made. In Chapter III all the ingredients were chosen because of their easy availability and capacity to produce a good, sound drink. But there are others, not quite so easily procurable but well worth the time and trouble to obtain. Let us analyse these materials, for by understanding them we shall have the control necessary to produce beers to our own particular requirements. This acquired knowledge will be the key to correct formulation, an essential part of the make-up of all brewers.

These examples might stiffen your resolve . . .! I know a bank manager in Lancashire who makes an excellent bitter and he transports the hard liquor (water) for it in an old milk churn from a well some thirty miles from his home. Another keen brewer often travels from Manchester to London to have a chat with a Southwark hop-factor. A colleague and I worked for nearly three years on a formulation to produce a dry stout. If you want something badly enough perseverance will usually get you through!

First water. This, certainly, is taken too much for granted by the student and amateur brewer, so it will not be amiss to define water and its relationship to brewing.

Water is generally classed for drinking purposes in the following six categories:

1. Rain water.
2. Upland surface water.
3. Surface water from cultivated land.
4. Shallow well water. (Less than 50 feet deep).
5. Deep well water.
6. Spring water.

There is a further classification on palatability:

1. Spring water   ⎫
2. Deep well water   ⎬ Wholesome.
3. Upland surface water   ⎭
4. Stored rain water
5. Surface water from cultivated land   ⎱ Suspicious
6. River water to which sewage has access ⎰ Dangerous.
7. Shallow well water

Modern breweries are invariably reliant on public water supplies which, thanks to the many water boards, supply a liquid which is entirely free from contagious infections.

Early brewers found that water drawn from the wells at Burton held preservative values, and bitter beers produced from it were far superior to bitters produced from other waters. Many years later, when the likes of Louis Pasteur interested themselves in the scientific aspects of winemaking and brewing, water, including the Burton well water, became the subject of analysis.

We now know that the quality of brewing water is determined on the following analysis. The total of dissolved organic and inorganic solids, chlorides, sulphates, nitrates, iron, hardness (temporary and permanent), and the quantity of organic matter. The latter being made up from some or all of the four elements, carbon, hydrogen, oxygen, and nitrogen. Whilst this book is not intended to be a highly scientific treatise it is felt that important data such as this should be highlighted so that the student will appreciate why brewers place great importance on having this knowledge.

Indeed, the character of any beer is influenced to a large degree by the liquor that is used. Now how do these hard and soft waters materialise? One has only to look at the side of a cliff and see the different strata of rocks, granites, chalks, and other minerals to find the answer. As the rain hits the earth it filters ever downwards, collecting particles of minerals en route.

Naturally the mineral substrata vary from district to district and therefore so do liquors. Thus we see that in the United States liquors around the Great Lakes are similar to Burton liquor. London liquors are softer by comparison, and therefore ideal for stout and mild ale production. The Birmingham and Manchester areas draw on lake water which is very soft. It is interesting to note how one can get vast variations in water qualities in one small area. The waters in the city of Glasgow are drawn from two sources, namely Loch Katrine and Gorbals. The hardness, expressed in parts per million, show this wide variation:

	Loch Katrine Water	Gorbals Water
Calcium hardness	5.0	36.0
Magnesium hardness	4.0	11.0
Total	9.0	47.0

The student can see that with slight adjustment Gorbals water will lend itself to the production of bitter, whilst the Loch Katrine water would be a good base for the brewing of lager.

One of the softest waters used is that of the Urquell Pilsner Brewery. Here the analysis shows that there are only 3 parts per 100,000 of solids. Compare this with Burton liquor which has about 60 parts per 100,000 of calcium sulphate.

As can be seen, it pays to have an analysis of any water used for brewing so that balance and quality control can be exercised.

The classification of water revolves around two main factors, alkalinity or acidity expressed as pH value. Alkalinity is due to larger proportions of hydroxyl ions, whilst acidity is due to large proportions of hydrogen ions. If we have a pH value of 7 it means that we have an equal amount of hydroxyl and hydrogen ions present—an even balance. The lower the pH, the lighter the acidity, thus the most acid of liquors has a value of 0, whilst the alkaline end of the scale will have a pH of 14; the lower the pH of the water the more the hydrogen ions increase over the hydroxyl ions. In many breweries today, as in many homes, ion exchange treatment is practised. This necessitates passing the liquor through a resin which removes the metal ions, then again through another resin which removes the acid ions present, the whole process resulting in a soft water. And the resins are regenerated by back washing with salt solution. On the other hand, as we shall see, acids can be added to acidify a carbonate water.

On analysis Burton water, whilst varying slightly at the wells of individual breweries, is found to contain the following, sulphate of lime, sulphate of magnesia, chloride of sodium, carbonate of magnesia, carbonate of iron, sulphate of potash, silica, and carbonate of lime. To Burtonise (or harden) a soft water the following formula can be employed.

4 parts gypsum
3 parts common salt
1 part sulphate of magnesia (Epsom salts)

This should be used at the rate of $\frac{1}{2}$ oz. per $4\frac{1}{2}$ gallons of liquor.

It must be pointed out that these ingredients are difficult to dissolve and it becomes necessary to boil them over a period, preferably with the hops. If a harder water is being employed then the formula must be modified slightly, in short, modify the formula to suit the water supplied in your area.

The brewing of stouts, and brown or mild ales requires water of a soft quality, or to be more exact, less hard than that used in Burton ales. Here again we have the material analysis of this type of water, which is common to London and Dublin. It is composed of alkaline chlorides, sulphate of lime, carbonate of lime, silica, oxide of iron, carbonate of magnesia, and organic matter. Since the beers produced with this type of water are of a dark nature absolute clarity is not so essential as with the waters used for bitter beers. Reference is again made to this point in the chapter on "Beer Types". In the search for soft water the student may be tempted to boil a hard liquor in the belief that it will become soft. This, unfortunately is a misconception. Boiled water does not soften completely and only a little of the hardness is removed. Continued boiling does not reduce the hardness further. Fresh rainwater is soft and can be used after taking the necessary precautions of boiling to eliminate any bacterial infection which may be present. It should be remembered that if boiling is resorted to a great deal of oxygen will be driven off so it is essential to reoxygenate the water by shaking or similar method. This will ensure that any yeast pitched will have the necessary oxygen to produce healthy growth. Some of us who live near to large airports have discussed the possibility of pollution to rainwater through kerosine vapours from aircraft. Up to the time of writing I have found no proof of pollution but the student would do well to bear in mind the possibilities of this happening, particularly in this day of ever enlarging aircraft and modification in fuels.

In the malting of grain the texture of the water is important. The first operation, known as "steeping" consists in soaking the grain in water for sufficient time to allow it to soften and assist in its germination. The German maltster and brewer uses soft water for this purpose which will yield a malt suitable for his brewing method, for his objective is to get a large amount of nitrogenous matter in his beer. His English opposite number prefers a hard water, for his need is to extract no more nitrogenous matter than is necessary to develop a healthy yeast growth during fermentation. It is a recognised fact that a soft water attacks and dissolves albuminous matter, whilst hard water gives it a toughness which extracts but little.

We have discussed at length the many types of waters used in brewing, their purity and faults. Occasionally however a "rogue" water will manifest itself and some thought must go into the cause of the fault or faults. Two examples are given which may be of interest to the student. If a brewing water is found to contain iron in any strength it should not be used. Iron, with the tannin from the hops, forms a black precipitate of tannate of iron which will give the beer a bad tint. Should this type of water inadvertently be used it can be largely removed by heating and mixing with powdered chalk. As it settles it carries down all but a slight trace of the iron. Sometimes one has to turn detective to trace a fault. After one lecture a lady came to me asking my advice on her brewing which, over a period of time, had produced cloudy, off-tasting beers. My questions elicited the facts that she used the same recipe, ingredients from the same source, the same strain yeast, and the same water supply. Further questions eliminated virtually all the ingredients, and I was left with a firm conviction that the answer to her problem was—Water. I asked if she could get water from a different supply to the one she normally used. It transpired that her sister used a different water. I recommended that she made her usual brew, using the same ingredients but using the water from her sisters supply. Some weeks later I received a delightful letter informing me that the problem was solved, and it had been, yes, you've guessed it; the water. It transpired that the supply eventually got so bad that office staff could not even make coffee, so the water board was approached. Their sleuths tracked the fault to a mains supply, which, when opened revealed a thick pad of fluoride which had clogged together, getting thicker and thicker, with the obvious results.

You may be asking yourself why these two examples have been quoted. It is for two reasons. The first is to warn you not to take anything for granted. Secondly, to be prepared to research, and make deductions, to ascertain the cause of any apparent shortcomings and mistakes. Never be too proud to seek advice or to communicate your theories to those who are a little more expert than yourself.

To sum up concerning liquor and its use in our beer making:

Old ale	
Bitter beers	
Barley wines	**Hard water.**
Dry and sweet stouts	
Mild ale	**Softer water.**
Lager	**Soft water.**

CHAPTER IV

Hops

There are two distinct types of hops. The Japanese Hop is indigenous to China, Japan, and neighbouring areas, but since it is devoid of lupulin it is useless for brewing purposes. The Common Hop is found in Europe and Western Asia and varieties of it are used extensively in the brewing industry. In England new varieties are constantly being developed, such as Density, Wye Challenger, Janus, Whitbreads Golding, Bramling Cross, Bullion, Wye Northdown, Defender. Older varieties include the Bramling hop, Canterbury Whitebine, Golding, Fuggles, Worcesters, and Colegates Hop. The main varieties favoured by British brewers are Fuggles, the Golding varieties, including the Whitbreads Golding Varieties, Challenger, Northern Brewer, and Bullion, which is a very robust and strong hop, capable of producing very bitter beers if not controlled. This is a very useful variety to have in producing that little extra bitterness when used in conjunction with say, Fuggles or one of the Goldings. Overseas hops include Yakimas, Oregon clusters, Oregon Fuggles, which

FUGGLES

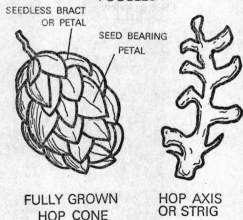

SEEDLESS BRACT OR PETAL

SEED BEARING PETAL

FULLY GROWN HOP CONE

HOP AXIS OR STRIG

are all American. From the continent of Europe we have Spalt, Hallertau, Tettnang, Hersbruck Gebirge, which are all German main crops. From Belgium we have Hallertau Setts, Brewers Gold, Saaz, and Northern Brewer, whilst Czechoslovakia produces Styrian Goldings, and Saaz as its main crops. It is probably superfluous to mention that these latter varieties are used extensively in the production of lager.

Why all these types and not just one? What are we looking for when we choose a particular kind of hop? To answer these questions let us look at the make up of a hop.

We can see on examination that the hop has two kinds of bracts or petals, which are seed bearing and seedless respectively. The petals are mounted on an axis or strig, "branches" of which feed the seed bearing and seedless petals. The other integral part of the hop is the corolla. Fully grown hop cones contain lupulin which is eventually transformed into an oily resinous content. The aroma—and bitterness of beer are largely due to this transformation. The aroma is that of a volatile essential oil, and the preservative power and bitter taste are derived from various resinous substances dissolved in the oil. The many varieties grown do vary appreciably in the balance between these essentials which they exhibit.

Think of a rose garden and its many varieties. All the flowers are roses, without doubt, but what a variation of scents and colours! Hops are the same, so let us know exactly what varieties suit our requirements and ask for them by name, and not just for a "pound of hops"—which may be of doubtful ancestry anyway.

Reputable hop factors will serve you well, but it is still worth knowing how to judge a good hop. If you purchase a packet of compressed hops, split the sample in half and a pale, yellowish green should be the colour running through the section. Should the colour be predominantly brown, like "autumn leaves", be suspicious for this can be old stock in which all the lupulin and essential oils have dissipated. It will therefore be useless for brewing. Similar symptoms will be observed if the hops have been packed in a damp or wet condition. In this case internal combustion takes place and the heat created ruins the oils and discolours the petals. If the colour appears sound take a few of the hops and rub them vigorously into

31

the palm of the hands for a short time. Allowing the hops to drop from the hands, sniff the palms and they should give off the full bodied bouquet of hops, free from any onion smell. Next rub the palms with the fingers and a sticky, resinous feeling should be experienced. Should these tests prove negative do not use the hops. It should be noted that hops deteriorate as they get older. This deterioration can be slowed down by keeping them well wrapped, in brown paper away from light and in a cool dry place with a temperature of 58° F.

Recommended varieties for the amateur or student are Fuggles or Goldings. These are fairly easily procured. The odd pack of Bullion or Northern Brewer is useful for blending purposes to produce that little extra bitterness in your pale ales. As lager demands a seedless hop, try a blend of the continental hops, including Saaz. These types may be a little more difficult to obtain, but are well worth hunting for. England, incidentally, is the only country to grow seeded hops. This was due, no doubt to a paper published in 1908 by Salmon and Amos entitled "On the value of the Male Hop", which stressed the importance and advantages to be had by ensuring the planting of male plants.

In Germany seeded hops were, and still are, frowned upon and in some districts it is an offence to produce a male crop. It would seem that the German and English approaches to the subject of hops were poles apart. The male hop is the larger of the species, and the English growers planted them for quantity, but the Germans and other continentals believed in the high quality of the female hop and so planted that.

As can be seen from the sketch the male, or seeded, hop is much larger than the seedless variety and therefore the yield per acre is much greater. However, to add to this state of confusion analysis shows that the seedless hops carry roughly twice the essential oil of the seeded variety. It has been mentioned that lager brewers use the seedless hops to attain these oils and thus confer the characteristic flavour upon this type of beer. With the ever increasing interest being shown in lager drinking more English brewers are turning their attention to the production of this drink. The importance of using seedless hops becomes apparent when we find that some 14,000 to

SEEDED   SEEDLESS

18,000 cwts are imported annually, and no doubt these figures will increase as the demand for lager increases, unless of course, the English growers can work out a formula for a balanced financial return for both seeded and seedless hop varieties. Since cost is a major factor in using seedless hops, many brewers, both English and continental, use seeded hops in the boiling in the copper to give the cleansing and preservative values, and then follow with the seedless variety after fermentation to give flavour and aroma.

It is acknowledged that there is still a lot to learn about the hop, and it should be pointed out that a vast amount of research is being undertaken by the Brewing Industry Research Foundation at Nutfield, and at Wye College and the East Malling Research Station.

The production of new varieties is carried out after deep study of the male and female to be used. There follows the crossing of these plants and raising the seedlings produced. The final stage is in the selection of the more healthy and useful plants for propagation purposes.

Another facet of research is in the attempt to produce varieties to replace the continental hops. For some years now triploid hops have been produced for research purposes. As they are virtually sterile there is a very low seed count. Unfortunately the essential oil content of these hops is not much higher than the normal seeded varieties. It is to be hoped that

33

this mystery can be solved, for if it can, the English hop growers, instead of decreasing, would thrive.

Research, thank heavens, does not stand still and hops, as we have seen, offer a wide field of study to the scientist. As a result of this we now have a useful additive in hop concentrate or extract. Here the essential oils and resins are extracted from the plant and concentrated by distillation. A leading company in this field, White Tomkins, and Courage, produce three types of concentrate.

1. Hopcon.
2. Essential oil of hops, to give hop aroma and flavour particularly in bottled beers.
3. Hop Natura, for giving hop aroma and flavour, also preservative resins to keep the beer sound.

This could be used to advantage when producing store beers such as barley wine. There are three grades of strength to be obtained. I have used these concentrates during fermentation and as an additive prior to bottling and have found them to be extremely efficient. A word of warning, though! The concentration is so high that great care should be taken in its application. Refrain, at all costs, from adding "one for the pot"! Should you decide to try hop concentrates there are certain rules you must observe. It is necessary to keep the concentrate cool and in a dry place away from light. The container should always be tightly screwed down. It is an advantage to transfer the contents to a smaller container when the original arrives at the half-way mark.

The blending of hops is practised by many breweries. Continental hops have a high resin content and full flavour. The bittering power of Bullion has already been mentioned. Saaz hops are lightly flavoured. There is a school of thought which suggests that seeds offer less aroma and lower resin content. No doubt this thought set in motion the latest development on the hop scene. "Hopstabil". This word symbolises yet another form of processed hops, but a process with a difference.

In 1966, after years of research and development the first Hopstabil plant was set in motion at Wolnzach in the midst of the Hallertau hop district of Germany.

The basics of this research was to provide a concentrate

with all the natural characteristics of the traditional hop as opposed to the chemically extracted hop syrup. The following aims were to be the criteria:

1. Stable quality.
2. Unadulterated product.
3. Reduced volume.
4. Easy handling.
5. Economic presentation.
6. No loss of bittering power during production.

After due examination of these items it was felt that a powdered hop would fulfil these six requirements. The research received encouragement and assistance from a number of eminent German breweries and the Weihenstephan School of Brewing. The success of this venture decided some of our oldest established hop factors to build a plant and go into production in England, and so Hop Developments Limited was formed in January 1969. The site chosen was Moor Farm, Eardiston, which lies roughly half way between Worcester and Tenbury Wells.

The plant receives and pulverises the hop into a fine powder form, thus breaking up the glands. This ensures a correct dispersal of the lupulin in the beer. Some breweries using dry hopping with conventional techniques have found that using Hopstabil a reduction of 75% can be achieved. The method of distribution also has great advantages, for being vacuum packed there is a reduction in transport costs. More important to the brewer is the fact that the vacuum packing ensures freshness, something the student should always bear in mind. Personally, having successfully used this form of hop, I think it will go from strength to strength, offering as it does so many advantages.

Another form is Hop Pelletisation, produced by an old illustrious company, Wigan Richardson & Company. These pellets are ideal for dry hopping, being $1\frac{1}{4}''$ in diameter, and weighing $\frac{1}{2}$ oz. I have used them in dry hopping barrelled draught beers, and have found them clean, simple and easy to use.

We have discussed the many forms of hop. Now what of its constituents? We talk of "bittering powers" and so on, which really does not tell us much, so let us take a much closer look.

Many years ago Payen and Chevallier, researching on hops, found that the main constituents were:

Volatile Oil   2.00%
Lupulin   10.30%
Resin   55.00%
Lignin   32.00%
Loss   .70%

Quite recently Dr. A. H. Cook, F.R.I.C., F.R.S., Director of the Brewing Industry Research Foundation, delivering a paper on "The Present Outlook on Hop Extracts" gave the hop composition in hop extracts as:

a–Acids (Humulones)   10–12%   (Wholly useful)
b–Acids (Lupulones)   4%
More complex and
  water soluble resins   3%   (Partly useful)
Essential Oil   1%
Tannins   (Doubtfully useful)
Cellulose   45%   (Insoluble and useless)
Protein   15%
Soluble carbohydrates   2%   (Useless as extract components)

From this we see that the hop is not just a cone of petals, but a highly complex combination of substances.

It is recognised that the alpha acid content in hops is important, being the forerunners of the real bittering agents. Indeed nowadays greater attention is being paid to the α–acid of hops. The following figures for the 1969 crop, for example, shows the variation of x–acid rate in different varieties.

Fuggles   Few below 4% and some well over 5%
Whitbread Goldings   5.6%–6.8%
Bramling Cross   Over 6%
Northern Brewer   7.5%–8.5%

Bullion offered a problem. Normally the alpha rate was around 8%–10% but the 1969 crop was only 5% and even below.

These figures vary from year to year according to climatic conditions prevailing during the growing of the crop. The region where the crop was grown will also be of the utmost importance. A Fuggles or Golding grown in Kent can have been grown in ideal conditions giving a high yield, whilst the yields from say, the Worcester yards, due to inclement weather, can be extremely poor. Therefore it pays to have an area of assessment of crops for the current year to ensure the purchase of quality.

Mention must be made here of the use of wild hops and growing hops from sets. The growing of hops is a specialised form of agriculture and the amateur and student should think very seriously of any grandiose ideas he may entertain of being a "mini-hop farmer". Like the growing of grapes, hop growing can be equally precarious, whilst wild hops could play havoc with your beer. So let us look at a hop grower at work, the pitfalls, headaches,—yes and heartaches, and I feel once these are known you will be happy to leave it to the expert.

At the outset he will have to decide the crop to be grown. Probably a disease-tolerant variety. Then a long walk round the fields to check the poles, wireworks, and maintenance, which will cost some £300 per acre. After planting vigilance is the key word, for his eye must be quick to spot the many diseases which can mar, and even wipe out, the crop. Frequent sulphur dusting and general good husbandry becomes the order of the day. You will note that he may be using a disease TOLERANT and not a disease RESISTANT strain. Such is this up-hill battle, fought with tolerant and not resistant strains. His other headaches include wet weather—too much and the hop yield is lowered. Then the crop can be attacked by mould, downy mildew, attacks of aphis, Virus and fungus diseases vie with verticillium, mosaic, and nettlehead to bring the grower to his knees. Still interested in growing hops? With any luck, plus expertise, the crop will be harvested—not by the armies of hop pickers as in days gone by. Alas, they are almost an extinct race. No, the picking will be done by highly sophisticated and expensive machines. The cost of these machines is heightened when you think of the very short period of the year in which they are employed. Once the harvest is completed the hops are taken to the oast house or kiln. This is invariably a round, brick built building surmounted by what looks like a cocks comb. The hops are spread over the floor and a fire, on which sulphur has been spread is lit. The heat and fumes dry and "cure" the hops and then escape through the "cocks comb". After curing they are packed in large bales called "pockets". After this they come under the scrutiny of the hop factor. Here the "trucker" will bring in a pocket for checking. The "examiner" will thrust a long, sharp knife into the pocket, cutting through an area. This happens twice more, covering the top, centre, and bottom of the pocket. His expert knowledge can tell from the cuts if the hops are correctly cured. A more modern method is the use of an electric moisture tester. Here two prongs are inserted into the pocket and an electric current passed over. Excessive moisture will give a high calibration and vice versa, in other words proving the degree of curing the hops. Following the "examiner" comes the "needleman" whose job is to sew up the sack after his predecessor. A "sampler" and foreman make up the team. The "sampler" will check the colour, rub, and nose in the manner already described.

As students and amateur brewers why not take a trip round the London hop area—Southwark? Try to make an appointment with one of the many hop factors and see at first hand this most interesting facet of brewing.

CHAPTER V

Malting and Milling

Grains such as wheat, oats, rye, and maize can all be used for malting purposes but barley is recognised as the finest grain for the preparation of malt. Some of the reasons are (a) Barley gives a malt which has no off-tastes or oily matter which can be found in other grains. (b) Barley germinates more quickly than other grains. (c) The growth of the acrospire takes place within the husk of the grain, thus protecting it from damage, as can happen to maize or wheat where the acrospire issues from the same part of the grain as the rootlets.

It is essential, in studying these details to know the break-down of a grain of barley and its subsequent development during germination.

In sketch 3 we see this break-down. It consists of two essential parts. (1) the endosperm and (2) the embryo, which as we see is made up of the scutellum, the rootlets, and the acrospire. The whole is encased in the testa or pericarp and sheathed in the palea.

The endosperm forms the main portion of the grain, in the region of 95–97%. If we view the starchy portion of the grain, the endosperm, we see that it terminates in an arch which is filled in with what appears to be a scar. This is the embryo. The scutellum on germination elongates, and growing between the testa and pericarp eventually forms the leaf and stalk, whilst the development of the radicle forms the roots.

In Sketch IV we see the development of the germinating barley. In (1) we note the growth of the root with a little development of the endosperm. In (2) there is a more vigorous root growth and starchy endosperm, whilst in (3) the grain is almost ready for the next stage in its life—that of being malted. But before this we should note the compositions of some grains and how their constituents vary.

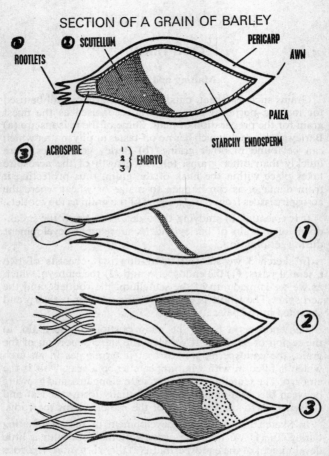

SECTION OF A GRAIN OF BARLEY

ROOTLETS
SCUTELLUM
PERICARP
AWN
PALEA
STARCHY ENDOSPERM
ACROSPIRE
1
2
3 EMBRYO

DEVELOPMENT AND CHANGE IN STARCHY
ENDOSPERM OF GERMINATING BARLEY

40

	Barley	Old Wheat	Maize	Rice
Water	12.0	11.1	11.5	10.8
Starch	52.7	62.3	54.8	78.8
Fat	2.6	1.2	4.7	0.1
Cellulose	11.5	8.3	14.9	0.2
Gum and Sugar	4.2	3.8	2.9	1.6
Albuminoids	13.2	10.9	8.9	7.2
Ash	2.8	1.6	1.6	0.9
Loss etc.	1.0	0.8	0.7	0.4
	100.0	100.0	100.0	100.0

This break-down is interesting reading and should be borne in mind, particularly when studying adjuncts and their relative evaluations when used in conjunction with barley in producing various types of beers.

It is thought by many people that the reason for malting is to convert the starch in the grain into sugar. Technically this is not so. Malting, primarily, is to develop the active soluble albuminous bodies which as they are developed there is also the production of a small quantity of sugar substances. Saccharification.

Malting consists of four processes or operations as: (1) Steeping. (2) Couching. (3) Flooring, and (4) Kiln-drying. In steeping the grain is soaked in water for sufficient time to enable it to draw in enough moisture to soften it, and to support its germination. As we have seen in the chapter on water the type and quality used is of paramount importance. Once the steeping is completed the water is drawn off and couching can begin. Here the grain is heaped on the floor in the form of a couch. The grain gradually heats up and germination commences. It begins to sweat and a pleasant smell begins to exude, after which the rootlet appears. At this point the maltster knows that it is time to break down the couch and spread the grain to a much lesser depth. Here begins the third operation when the grain is said to be "on the floor". The depth of grain can vary from 4–12 inches, according to the weather or season in old maltings. In modern buildings ideal conditions are simulated. The grain is turned every four to five hours so that it might all receive the same benefits and conditions of light, heat, and moisture. This allows the germination to proceed uniformly through the mass.

A strict watch is kept on the growth of the acrospire or plumule, which is allowed to grow to varying lengths according to the beer to be produced. As a general rule it is allowed to grow from two thirds to three quarters of the length of the grain. Where raw grain is used the acrospire should be grown almost to the full length of the grain so that the maximum amount of diastase may be developed. In stout or porter production the plumule is stopped at half the length of the grain so that the malt, when mashed will yield a dextrinous wort, which will give a full mouthed beer. Care must be taken to ensure that the acrospire does not extend beyond the end of the grain or a waste of starch materials will occur. When the growth has reached its required length the grain is thinned out and germination ceases. Now the fourth operation, that of kiln drying, may commence. It is at this point that the grain comes to the parting of the ways for it is malted at varying temperatures to produce the many types and styles of beer we drink. The types of malt produced are:

Lager malt. As the name implies used in lager production. Is less modified than pale malt.

Pale malt. The base for most British beers. Roasted at temperatures ranging from 120° F, to as high at 140° F.

Crystal and Amber malt. Roasted similarly but having a final temperature of 160–170° F. The colours are self explanatory.

Brown malt. Is roasted at temperatures ranging between 180–200° F.

Black or Patent malt. This is prepared by roasting in cylinders. A rule of thumb method worth remembering. The darker the colour the more flavour but less fermentable matter. Conversely the lighter the colour the more fermentable matter. It therefore becomes obvious that a blend of malts is required in some beers to get balance, gravity and flavour.

Although this chapter deals with the malting process it would be appropriate to mention the non-malted grains which are used in conjunction with malt. These are collectively known as raw grains, but are generally referred to as adjuncts. They

42

are mostly kiln dried at various temperatures but remain unmalted. Their main use in the commercial field is to reduce brewing costs and vary flavour characteristics. When used wth malt a chain reaction occurs, for as the malt conversion takes place it begins to react on the unmalted grain where the starch is also converted. The student should be wary in the use of adjuncts confining their use to around 5% for light beers and 12% of the total grains used for heavy beers. The more popular adjuncts are Barley (dry), Torrified Barley, Wheat, Maize, Oats, Bran, Rye, and Rice. Again these can be used in the form of grain, syrup, or flakes, these last two being the easiest to use. Should grain be used it should be crushed, when it becomes known as grit, then boiled for some time before adding to the wort.

To simulate the malting conditions a large deep sided tray is ideal, being the one receptacle for Steeping, Couching, and Flooring. The kilning process can be completed in the oven, but first make sure that you can control the temperatures required accurately.

Finally, how does one recognise a good malt? On examination it should be plump, full and thin skinned which will yield more starch than a small, thin variety. It should be crisp, and easily broken. If drawn across a dark surface it should leave a chalky line. If cracked by the teeth it should not have that extreme hardness known as steeliness or flintiness. Should the malt be shrivelled the barley was probably cut before it was ripe, too sudden a heat was applied on the kiln during the malting process, or bad weather affected it. Mention should be made here of a new adjunct material recently developed and tried by the American brewing industry. This is the use of Sorghum grits in the production of American type lager. The Sorghums, the cereal grains from which grits are milled, have their origin in India and Africa. They were among the earliest wild plants to be cultivated and were shipped to America by the slave traders in the early 1800's.

There are many types of cultivated plants, ranging from 2 to 5 feet tall. The blossoms mature into as many as 2,000 seeds. In Africa these are fermented into a beverage known as kaffir beer. One American brewery used 40% sorghum with no harmful effect to taste, shelf life, etc., of the resultant beers.

Experiments have proved that Sorghum is every bit as efficient as maize, and cheaper to use. Perhaps it will not be too long before we find this commodity on the British market.

We now come to the milling of the grain. "It's all grist to the mill" runs the old saw, and this comes from the days when the government taxed the grain and not the beer as is the case today. Certain unscrupulous individuals worked a nice little fiddle by "stretching" the dutiable grain with such things as beans; as far as the mill was concerned it was all grist or milled grain.

It should be remembered that the milling and size of the grist is very important—this operation is not like flour milling, where the husk is separated from the flour. In brewing, if the malt is too finely ground the fine powder can block the holes of the false bottom of the mash tun. Fine grist can also cause "balling", the grain coagulating into balls. The effect of this in both cases is loss of extraction. Similarly a grain which has not been ground finely enough will also cause loss of extraction. A fine grist gives the best extraction, therefore we should experiment to obtain a correct mesh size for the false bottom of our mash tun to overcome the problem of clogging. Balling can be overcome by SLOWLY shaking the grist on to the liquor, as opposed to pouring it on.

There are several mills, of different designs, on the market. One looks and operates like a mincing machine, grinding the grain to a set grist size. Another type, electrically operated, uses fast rotating cutters. It is adjustable to give various grist sizes. Lastly, there is a hand operated mill, where the grain is inserted into the top and is funnelled on to two stainless steel rollers which can be pre-set to give the required grist size. As the grain is crushed between the two rollers the grist drops into a container and is then ready for use.

CHAPTER VI

Yeast

Yeast is one of the most important ingredients to brewers and winemakers alike and one least understood by amateurs. First, what is yeast, and how does it function? A yeast cell is about 1/5000th of an inch in size and reproduces itself by budding. Each cell buds three times, and each of the three buds buds off three more, and so on. Research has proved that it is not the yeasts that create the ferments but substances in them called enzymes or ferments. In one cell there may be a thousand different enzymes.

Louis Pasteur advanced the theory that the reason for the prolific growth of yeast lay in the fact that it required the oxygen from the sugar in order to live. It was not until 1942 that Myerhof proved that what fermentation provides the yeast cell with is not oxygen but energy. So much for functional technicalities.

And now varieties. As in all things in life there are "good" and "bad" yeasts, so let us look at the former. In brewing two main types of yeast are used. These are the "High" sketch 5 and 6 and "Low" sketch 7 and 8 yeasts. In simple parlance the "High" yeast cells rise to the surface of the fermenting liquid, whilst the "Low" yeast cells sink to the bottom of the fermenting container. For the more academically minded, and as a point of reference, they are grouped under two main headings, *saccharomyces cerevisiae*, which is a top fermenting yeast, and *saccharomyces carlsbergensis*, which is a bottom fermenting yeast. It was used in Munich and was known to produce excellent beers. In the middle of the 19th. century J. Jacobsen, a brewer with the Carlsberg brewery, with this knowledge in mind, visited the Spaten brewery in Munich and returned to Copenhagen with some of this yeast, which had been carefully cooled each time that the coach stopped. It was this yeast that Emil Hansen successfully isolated a pure cell, and from it grew a pure strain in sufficient quantities to pitch on to a normal brewery wort. Thus today we are indebted to these two gentlemen for the research and production of one of the finest strains of yeast used in brewing.

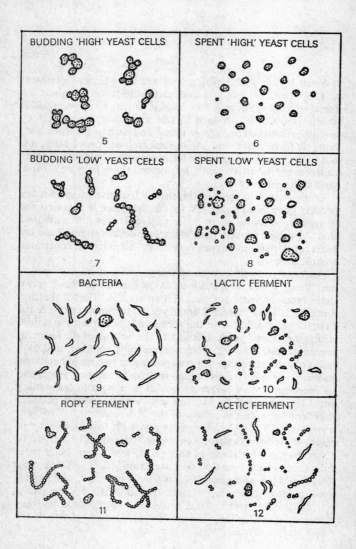

BUDDING 'HIGH' YEAST CELLS	SPENT 'HIGH' YEAST CELLS
5	6
BUDDING 'LOW' YEAST CELLS	SPENT 'LOW' YEAST CELLS
7	8
BACTERIA	LACTIC FERMENT
9	10
ROPY FERMENT	ACETIC FERMENT
11	12

Hansen studied the formation of six types of yeast which he classified thus:

1. **Sacch. pastorianus I.** A bottom fermenting yeast, offering strong, bitter taste to beers.
2. **Sacch. pastorianus II.** A feeble top working yeast, found in the air in breweries. It is not associated with disease in beer.
3. **Sacch. pastorianus III.** A top working yeast which will produce yeast turbidity.
4. **Sacch. ellipsoidius I.** A bottom fermenting yeast, occurring on the outside of grapes.
5. **Sacch. ellipsoidius II.** A bottom working yeast, separated from turbid beer, and capable of producing yeast turbidity.
6. **Sacch. cerevisiae.** An English top working yeast.

The student of yeast may become a little perplexed when he reads for instance, that sacch cerevisiae causes beer spoilage, and then is told in the same breath that this is the "High" yeast used in English breweries. Or that sacch. Carlsbergensis is the excellent yeast strain used in the production of lager, and a little later on reads that sacch. Carlsbergensis causes haze in draught beers. All very confusing, so let us here and now put this to rights by saying that the naming of yeasts is a botanical matter, and experiments to classify yeasts do not take into account whether or not they will cause spoilage. Similarly wild yeasts can cause the student to scratch his head, when he reads that sacch. Carlsbergensis and sacch. cerevisae are wild yeasts. Let us look therefore into how this apparent contradiction comes about. There are many varieties of yeast found in breweries. A wild yeast is one alien to the production of a certain type of beer. The following example will illustrate this point. Sacch. cerevisae would be a wild yeast if present during the production of lager. Conversely sacch. Carlsbergensis would be a wild yeast if present in a top fermenting brewery. There are, of course, many other wild yeasts but it is felt that the explanation of the example will help the student to put the record straight.

The amateur is rather fortunate in having a sound choice of "High" and "Low" yeasts at his disposal. A visit to your local wine and brewing stockists will show a selection of beer yeasts produced by different laboratories. They can be obtained in four forms. (1) In granular form. (2) In tablet form. (3) In liquid form, (4) an agar slant. Some years ago I did some research into these forms and the liquid forms were the purest. They are obtained in small phials where one sees a small amount of yeast laying in a liquid which is usually a nutrient which is to assist the yeast to activate. Other sources of supply are the White Shield Worthington, and the Guinness Special Stout. These are bottle matured beers and each bottle contains a small amount of yeast. To obtain a culture is quite simple—nay, a pleasure! Drink the beer, ensuring that the sediment at the bottom of the bottle has been retained. Into a thoroughly sterilised bottle put sugar water (1 oz. sugar dissolved in 4 fl. oz. water) and a small amount of malt extract. Pour into this liquid the sediment from the beer, plug the neck of the bottle with cotton wool, and place in a warm temperature of about 70° F. After two or three days bubbles will be seen rising in the bottle and this means that the yeast is activated and growth is taking place. When thoroughly activated, pitch on to the prepared wort. The same procedure is observed if yeast cultures are bought. Should you be unable to purchase a beer yeast culture then there is a substitute. Try a perlschaum or champagne yeast. It is a good sedimentary yeast and can be used quite successfully in beer production.

The student should not make the mistake of thinking that all beers are made with single strain yeasts. Scientists in brewing have developed and are still developing new techniques in the use of yeasts. Yeast mutation and blending can result in better flavours, greater stability, more polished products, and so on. It is a fact that many brewers today use over 20 different strains of yeast when pitching. Another technique is to divide the wort into two known quantities and pitch on to one a "Low" yeast, and a "High" on to the other. After the completion of the primary fermentation both beers are blended so that a good secondary fermentation can ensue. Naturally the amateur does not have the laboratory facilities at his disposal to effect the accurate control practised in the breweries, but he should experiment, within his capabilities, with yeast blending, not only to gain initial experience, but to prove to himself that these methods do provide changes in the beer. Notes should be kept of types and amounts blended and the results obtained. Should the two yeast system be tried remember that it is essential that the two yeasts and fermentations are kept separate until blending takes place. It is probably superfluous, but necessary to stress the importance of having sterile conditions at all times to avoid the chances of infection and contamination from other organisms.

Let us now descend into the chamber of yeast horrors, for at the beginning of this chapter it was mentioned that there are "baddies" and well as "goodies"! One thing to guard against is autolysis. This is a natural process following the death of the yeast cell, for the cell disintegrates and can put off-flavours and tastes into the beer. With regular racking this should not be experienced.

The following are slime forming yeasts. *Hansenula anomala, pichia membranaefaciens, candida albomarginata, pullularia pullulans, rhodotorula mucilaginosa*. The symptoms are easily diagnosed, for the beer pours with an oil-like viscosity, whilst the bead slowly ascends to the top of the glass. Needless to say it is a highly contagious contamination and like others of its kind needs drastic measures to eradicate it. First, pour away the whole batch down a drain and flush it with a strong disinfectant. *All* equipment that was in contact with the brew, such as bottles, stoppers, siphon tubes, bulk fermenters, filters, funnels, (and don't forget the air lock if it was used) should all be treated in a strong solution of bleach or similar sterilising agents. Wash thoroughly in hot water afterwards.

The species *brettanomyces* cause spoilage in bottled beers, and one of the worst, *brettanomyces bruxellensis* produces flavours which are harsh and off-flavoured.

Another horror is a ropy ferment, (see sketch 11) which is another contagious disease, capable of being spread to other beers. Whilst sketch 11 depicts the disease as viewed under a microscope, if left unchecked it will be visible to the naked eye. As can be seen it is identified as strings of spherical cells suspended in the brew. Hence the term rope. The sugars are converted into a dextrin-like gum and carbon dioxide gas, the combination of which results in a viscous, gummy liquid. It thrives best at a temperature of 86° F.

Lactic ferment. (Sketch 10). The yeasts are identified as small, elliptical forms which appear to develop in neutral and alkaline solutions at a temperature of 95° F.

Acetic ferment. (Sketch 12). These are rod-like cells capable of turning a brew into vinegar with great rapidity. Malt vinegar of course, is produced in this manner. Ideal temperature—86° F.

Vibrios. Resemble bacteria (sketch 9) and are the chief formers of putrefaction caused through very bad conditions.

Again, it emerges with startling clarity that hygiene is all-important. Cleanliness and sterilisation of equipment must at all times be exercised to eliminate the chance of these many contagions. Louis Pasteur points out that in Spring, Summer, and Autumn the difficulty in preserving yeasts is increased by the higher temperatures prevailing, whilst in the early part of the Autumn the materials used in brewing are covered with a variety of parasites.

Despite our shudderings at the last thoughts, a ray of light emerges when we find that yeasts are capable of being purified, so the following methods of purifying yeast may be of interest.

(1) A small amount of wort, to which $1\frac{1}{2}\%$ tartaric acid and 2–3% of alcohol has been added. Successive growths in this medium will help purify the yeast, though it will not eliminate *sacch. pastorianus*.

(2) Boil water with 10% sugar and 0.2% tartaric acid and place in a sterilised bottle, leaving plenty of air space. Pitch on yeast when the temperature is 75° F. It has been found that the principal disease ferments found in beers are checked in their development by the presence of air, as they are favoured by its absence.

(3) Cultivate the yeast in wort and to every 100 cc., add 10–12 drops of a 10% aqueus solution of carbolic acid.

(4) Yeast, particularly "Low" yeast, can be purified by growth at low temperatures, since these temperatures are prejudicial to the development of disease ferments, which rarely appear at a lower temperature of 50° F, and cease to be active at this temperature.

A few observations regarding yeast and fermentations as practised in the leading breweries should be of help to the student.

Fermentations can take place at temperatures ranging from 32–130° F, the most rapid ones occurring at 77–86° F, but in brewing the blest range is from 58–68° F. The temperature at which the fermentation is conducted has a distinct influence on the flavour of the beer. The best flavours are produced by a slow, continuous fermentation brought about by keeping to low temperatures. For instance, The old Burton brewers kept their temperatures at between 57–70° F, for their fine ales. Common ales are pitched to work at slightly higher temperatures. It is worth remembeong that active yeast in full ferment creates heat which can destroy these fine flavours' hence the use of cooling systems by the brewers to offset this happening. So you will see by this that it is essential to maintain some form of temperature control during fermentation.

CHAPTER VII

Sugars, Carbohydrates and Albuminoids

Many types of sugars and caramels are used in the brewing industry. It can generally be accepted that most sugars are "invert", i.e. ordinary sugar that has been hydrolysed with a dilute acid, an operation which changes the sucrose in the sugar into equal parts of laevulose and dextrose.

Other methods of inverting sugars should be studied. Under natural conditions when ordinary sugar is added to a brew the yeast will proceed to invert it prior to carrying on with the fermentation. Alternatively, ordinary sugar can be partially inverted by boiling for a short time after tartaric acid has been added, on a ratio of three pounds of sugar to $\frac{1}{8}$ oz. tartaric acid. A point here which may be of assistance in your formulations. If three pounds of sugar has been liquefied in $1\frac{1}{2}$ pints of water the resultant gravity should be 300°. Sugar can also be inverted by high diastase malt extract providing the solution does not exceed 150° F, the ideal conversion temperature being 131° F.

There are different types of brewing sugars. Some of them may have little use in today's commercial field but the amateur can well experiment with them occasionally in the hope that in his formulations he may discover a beer which would be described as the veritable elixir of life!

Loaf, Havannah, Bastards, Demerara, Jaggery, Trinidad, Black treacle, Golden syrup, and Molasses are all forms of sugar that were, or still are being used in different forms of brewing. Care must be exercised in the use of most of them, particularly in the last three mentioned, on account of the strong flavours they confer on the beer. It would be wiser to use them in conjunction with the ordinary invert, cane, or beet sugars until the required balance is reached. The use of molasses must be extremely limited owing to the pungent off-flavours which can be imparted to the brew.

Caramels play a big part in some brewing, and are made by heating sugar to temperatures above 410° F. This is an industry in its own rights, and one well known company produces over 80 different types of caramel. These range from light caramel used by the distilleries to colour whiskey, to caramel used by pickle manufacturers to tempt your eye and palate into trying their pickled onions. Caramels are used for wine and cider colouration, and in certain stouts, and liquid gravy browning is nothing more than caramel. Malt is also caramelised and used in certain brewing operations. A sweet stout can be made by using a Silcose caramel, and if you have difficulty in obtaining black and chocolate malt for a dry, or Irish type stout, use Intense caramel. These items can be obtained from Lamberts of Uxbridge.

Glucose can also be used in brewing quite satisfactorily, especially in producing sweet stouts and brown ales. Remember, though, that in place of every pound of sugar you will need to use one and a quarter pounds of glucose.

Another form of sweetening is Lactose, or milk sugar, and it can be thoroughly recommended, together with liquid saccharin, available as "sweetex". The advantage of these two is that they are non-fermentable, and are therefore ideal for producing sweet stouts, brown ales, and certain types of barley wine. One can thus bring any drink, wine or beer to the required sweetness without fear of a secondary fermentation being started.

Some companies who specialise in brewing sugars, produce special syrups to suit certain types of beers, such as a caramel syrup with a small amount of liquorice in it, used in the production of a brown ale.

Similarly, one can purchase priming syrups. These are, as the name implies, added to the bottle or barrel after fermentation to produce the carbon dioxide gas to give the sparkle required.

Finally, honey can be used, preferably in strong bitters. Here it is best to try a small "pilot" brew, on two counts (a) to get the correct balance, and (b) to see if you like it! After all, flavours produced from honey do not suit all palates. I have tried this type of beer and found it to be a good, wholesome, drink, but the palate seemed a little perplexed at what it was receiving. This, no doubt, was a psychological reaction after drinking an ordinary bitter but before dashing out to buy your honey I strongly recommend that you read what I have to say on honey beer in the chapter dealing with beer types.

Under the two headings of carbohydrates and albuminoids we have starchy matters, cereal grains, different types of sugars, and even flesh. It will be readily understood then, that the maintenance of life in human and animal form is due to the many forms under the terms of Carbohydrates and Albuminoids. As we shall see the production of beer is greatly influenced by these two items.

Carbohydrates are so named because basically they consist of carbon, oxygen, and hydrogen in proportions which form water.

On the other hand albuminoids, whilst having an inferior position to carbohydrates, are of the utmost importance in brewing. They nourish the yeast, and are starch converting, or natural saccharifying agents. Albuminoids have the same three elements as carbohydrates, carbon, hydrogen, and oxygen, plus a fourth, nitrogen.

We find that carbohydrates and albuminoids are in many ways direct contrasts. Carbohydrates, if pure, do not oxidise or decay, and are unaffected by the action of moisture and air; they also yield heat. Albuminoids easily undergo change, and they supply the material for the development of parts which uses the power obtained from heat.

With albuminoids we need only concern ourselves with three types or varieties.

1. *Albumin*, which occurs in wheat, rye, potatoes, egg whites, and plants. It is soluble in water, and is precipitated by water.

2. *Fibrin or Gluten*. The former is usually applied to this nitrogenous matter when obtained from animal sources, whilst gluten is that obtained from the vegetable kingdom. It is found in all cereals in varying amounts, oats having the largest percentage, rice the least, and wheat and barley being half way between.

3. *Casein or Legumin*. Here again casein is applied to materials from mineral sources whilst legumin refers to that obtained from the vegetable kingdom. Both are found in milk, beans and peas.

With carbohydrates we need only consider three groups for our practical needs.

The first group consisting of: cellulose, starch, and dextrin.

The second group consisting of: cane sugar, and maltose.

The third group consisting of: two glucoses, dextrose, and laevulose.

Cellulose and starch are insoluble in the cold, whilst the remainder are dissolved by water.

Cellulose is the main bulk of wood and the framework of all plants. Starch is found in nearly all plants. It is the pith of a variety of palms which we call sago, we find it in the potato, and in seeds such as the cereals. Starch is a white, tasteless, odourless substance. It is insoluble in water, alcohol or ether. If heated when dry to 160° C no change will take place, but if heated to 160–200° C it is converted to a substance, soluble in cold water, called dextrin. Above these temperatures it will decompose. Now if starch is heated with water we find great changes will take place. If we heat from 45–90° C the granules will swell and burst, and the cell contents will merge with the water to form a translucent or semi-fluid, according to the proportions of starch and water used. This fluid is called starch paste.

Here, then, we begin to see the reasons for mashing grain, for it is after this production of starch paste that we go on to convert it to maltose and dextrin, i.e. to brewing sugars.

Cane Sugar (or Saccharose) is the most important of the group of carbohydrates. In its crystallised form it is half as heavy again as water. At a temperature of 160° C it melts without loss of weight, but slightly above this temperature changes occur, resulting in a conversion into the two other sugar forms, namely laevulose and dextrose. At 210° C and above as we have already discovered, cane sugar is converted to caramel.

We know that invert sugar consists of a mixture of equal weights of dextrose and laevulose and it will help our studies if we analyse each of these bodies.

Laevulose is an uncrystallisable, colourless syrup, as sweet as cane sugar and showing similar general chemical properties to those of dextrose. It is less controlled by the action of alkalies and ferments, but more readily undergoes change under the action of heat and acids.

Laevulose is as sweet as cane sugar, but dextrose is only half as sweet. Therefore invert sugar will possess three quarters the sweetness of cane sugar, whilst ordinary glucose or dextrin alone is one third less sweet. Brewing with cane or invert sugar will produce a sweeter wort than if glucose is used and this difference will be made stronger in the finished beer.

It should now be obvious that sugars should be given every consideration in conjunction with the other ingredients when making our formulation for a specific style of beer.

CHAPTER VIII

Mashing and Sparging

Before we can discuss the merits of mashing and sparging it is necessary to have a container in which we can perform this operation. In English brewing we employ the Infusion system where a vessel called the mash tun is used. This is a large container which has a false bottom which is perforated like a colander. This prevents the grist from sinking to the bottom of the mash tun and so leaves a clear wort. Another important item in the mash tun is the paddle or paddles. These rotate in the tun, thoroughly stirring the mash to ensure the maximum release from the grain. This is known as "paddling the goods (grist)", or "rousing". The paddles are not usually employed throughout the mash, but at intervals. When the paddles are not in use the goods are said to be "resting". So we have resting and rousing. When the wort is run off the grist lays on the false bottom of the tun. Now this grist still has residual sugars which have to be washed out, so a finely perforated, rotating arm, emitting a fine spray of hot water is used. This is known as "sparging". So now knowing what is involved we must emulate the mash tun in miniature form. Nowadays it is possible to buy a container for mashing, but the two examples I give have been used by me and with great success, so to that extent they are practical.

In sketch 13 a stainless steel tea urn has been modified to use as our mash tun. The support legs for the false bottom were made from stainless steel and rivetted at the centre so that they could close like scissors. This enables them to go through the narrow aperture at the lid, to be opened when inside. The false bottom is a fairly coarse mesh gauze capable of keeping the grist from falling through. This too, is on a frame, hinged to allow it to pass through the narrow neck. When in situ it should fit snugly against the side of the urn. The agitator pipe is a piece of $\frac{1}{8}''$ or $\frac{1}{10}''$ bore tube, preferably stainless steel. It should be long enough to protrude through the drilled insulation at the top of the urn, formed to an "L" bend at the base, and finally formed into a ring of $6\frac{1}{2}''$ diameter. The end of the ring is nipped together to seal it off and a series of $\frac{1}{16}''$ holes,

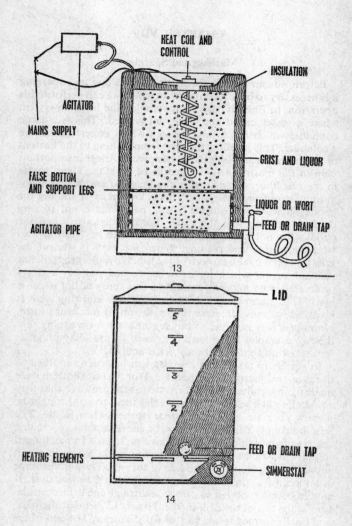

HEAT COIL AND CONTROL

INSULATION

AGITATOR

MAINS SUPPLY

GRIST AND LIQUOR

FALSE BOTTOM AND SUPPORT LEGS

LIQUOR OR WORT

AGITATOR PIPE

FEED OR DRAIN TAP

13

LID

5

4

3

2

HEATING ELEMENTS

FEED OR DRAIN TAP

SIMMERSTAT

14

$\frac{1}{2}''$ apart are drilled round round the full periphery of the ring. As can be seen in sketch 13 the pipe runs along the wall of the urn and its base and the ring covers the centre to give maximum agitation to the grist and liquor.

A piece of P.V.C. tubing is attached from the top of the agitator pipe to the agitator. Now this device is nothing more than a fish tank aerator which pumps air via a rubber diaphragm, and can be purchased from most pet shops. The heater in sketch 13 is an ordinary immersion heater to which is fitted a thermostat with a range of 0–190° F which is ideal for our requirements. Most of these thermostats are not wholly accurate and one should do some trials, with the aid of an accurate thermometer and mark on the thermostat scale the positions of our required heats.

Sketch 14 is an ordinary stainless steel wash boiler with the heater elements at the base. The variable switch of Medium, High, and Low is no good for our needs and has to be replaced with a simmerstat. These can be salvaged from an old electric cooker or purchased from any reputable electric factor. The scale reads from Off, to On, and graduates from 1 to 4 and eventually to Full. Again, trials should be resorted to and the scale marked as before. Naturally we should use the agitator, pipe, support legs and false bottom. In both cases the capacity is 5 gallons.

Having got our mash tun operational let us put it to work. But first, what is mashing and, more important, *why* do we mash? We know that malt comprises maltose and dextrin which are released from the grain when immersed in hot water at various temperatures. These temperatures are critical in producing worts of different balance, hence the need for mashing.

Needless to say mashing is a very intricate process with many complex physical and chemical changes taking place. We know that we break down the starch in the malt into carbohydrates, the major portion being used by the yeast to carry on its form of life and in so doing producing alcohol. It also produces some unfermentable carbohydrates which are of the greatest importance in producing character to the beer. It is important therefore that in mashing we should not attempt to break down all the carbohydrate material, but at the end of the mash we should have a ratio of fermentable and non-fermentable substances left in the wort. We should also remember that the alpha and beta amylases are sensitive to destruction by heat so the brewer must always bear in mind suitable extract temperatures. In English brewing we find that the temperatures of 135–150° F produce the right conditions for beers and stouts consumed in this country.

At this juncture it may be as well to explain the different forms of mashing used in brewing. They consist of the Infusion system as used in English brewing, and the Decoction system as practised on the continent of Europe. There are modifications to these systems as in some American breweries where they use a combination of the two, but we can disregard these rarer forms. The Infusion system really means mashing at one temperature, whereas the Decoction system involves mashing at various temperatures. Why two? Why can't they use just one? The answer in one word is PALATE. Over the centuries the British and Continentals have developed their own particular tastes for drinks produced by the two systems. The infusion system produces Porters, Stouts, Store or Export beers which require a large part of dextrin to maltose in the wort to get the full characteristic taste. It is also essential for store or export beers to offset any tendency to develop acidity. Weak, sweet beers on the other hand require a high maltose and low dextrin ratio. So if our mash temperatures range from 135–150° we should bear in mind that the lower the temperature the more Maltose we produce, the higher the temperature the higher the Dextrin content.

As it is the ratio of maltose to dextrin which fundamentally helps to establish the character of a beer it is interesting to study the following tables of an experiment conducted many years ago on the effect of mashing time. A mash was made using 10 parts by weight of water to 1 part of malt at a temperature of 145° F. It will be noted that the yield after two hours was very slight.

Time of Infusion	Maltose	Dextrin	Total %	Ratio: Maltose to Dextrin
½ hour	48.60%	14.61%	63.21	3.3 to 1
1 hour	52.35%	12.26%	64.61	4.2 to 1
2 hour	53.56%	11.39%	64.95	4.7 to 1
3 hour	54.60%	11.05%	65.65	4.9 to 1
7 hour	61.47%	3.53%	65.00	17.4 to 1

Similarly the effect of the QUANTITY of water used, to a given amount of malt at a maintained temperature of 140° F, for two hours produced these results.

Ratio: Malt/ Water	Maltose	Dextrin	Total %	Ratio: Maltose to Dextrin
1 to 10	53.56%	11.39%	64.95	4.7 to 1
1 to 5	49.99%	12.92%	62.91	3.8 to 1
1 to 2	49.00%	13.88%	68.88	3.5 to 1
1 to 1	46.80%	15.08%	61.88	3.1 to 1

As can be seen the greatest yield of maltose and dextrin came from the greatest quantity of water.

Naturally the quality of the grain used will vary these figures but the examples given illustrate the importance of mashing times and water quantities.

During mashing tests have to be made to see if the conversion is complete and that no starch remains. The test is quite simple, and is known as the yellow spot, or iodine test. One places a small amount of the wort onto a white saucer and adds a drop of iodine. If starch is present the iodine will react by turning a deep purple-blue. If no starch is present the iodine will remain yellow. This is the signal to run off the wort and commence sparging.

The secret of sparging lies in the fineness of the spray. If the sparging liquor is allowed to drop on to the grist like rain it will cake together and the liquor will be unable to run through. For our purposes we can use a watering can with a very fine rose, making sure that it has not recently been used for watering in weed killer! A lesson here: equipment used for brewing should be kept wholly for brewing. Another idea is to use a garden spray to which is added a pump. This is ideal, for it has an adjustable spray, ranging from a mist to a heavy spray. Remember that the sparging liquor should be 20° F hotter than the final mash temperature. If we finalised the mash at 150° F, then the sparging liquor should be 170° F.

Let us collate what we have learned so far by making a typical infusion mash, which will eventually be transformed into a bitter beer. The volume will be 5 gallons. The liquor, ideally hard, is put into the mash tun and the heater is set in motion to bring it up to 145° F. The grist has been prepared by a fine grind of 8¾ lb. of pale malt, to which has been added 1¼ lb. of flaked maize as the adjunct. The grist is added to the liquor slowly to avoid "balling" as has been mentioned in chapter 3. The agitator is set in motion allowing the goods to be stirred. To assist in speeding up the conversion 2–3 oz. of malt extract may be added. If, however, you have a liquid diastase, use 1 oz. in preference. During the mash period switch off the agitator from time to time to allow the goods to rest. It is a good thing to cross check your temperature with a thermometer from time to time. Do an iodine test and note the gradual change from the purple-blue, to a reddish brown and violet, and finally to the pure yellow spot. At this point the wort is run off, leaving the grist on the false bottom of the mash tun. The sparging liquor is brought up to 165° F, transferred to the spray and sparging is carried out. Check with an accurate short range hydrometer and when a reading of .004 is reached this can be said to be the end of the sparge for all practical purposes.

Let us now turn to the decoction form of mashing. In infusion mashing we have seen that only the mash tun is employed to complete the mash. In decoction mashing two vessels are employed, for in addition to the mash tun a vessel called the Lauter Tun is used. The beer produced by this method is of course, lager. The fine flavours developed in this beer are to a large extent the result of decoction mashing, although there are other factors which contribute, as we shall see. We have said that the decoction process entails making the use of more than one temperature. Thus, if we boil part of the mash and add this to the remainder, that is termed a decoction.

We have double decoction; three mash, four temperature; and the old Bavarian methods of Lautermaisch, or light or thin mash; and Dickmaisch or thick or heavy mash. Due to modern economics many breweries employ single, double, or three mash, four-temperature systems. These various systems are worthy of detailed explanation.

A single decoction usually has a starting temperature of 120–130° F and is then increased to 170–175° F. It is usual to add adjuncts which are boiled with a small amount of malt until they reach a gelatinised state. When added to the mash they act as a nitrogen dilution for the malt.

For a double decoction the grits and about 17% of the malt are mashed at 126° F then immediately raised to boiling. At the same time the malt is mashed in the mash tun at the same temperature. The two are then blended and held at 153° F for $\frac{3}{4}$ of an hour. A third of the mash is drawn off and boiled and returned to the bulk. This raises the temperature to 172° F. This is allowed to settle before running off the main wort and sparging. Run off times should be three to four hours.

Three mash, four temperatures. In this system the liquor is flooded on to the grist COLD. The temperature is then raised to 100° F and mashing proceeds for a short period, after which part of the wort is drawn off and boiled for 10–15 minutes and then returned to the mash tun, to produce a temperature of about 120–130° F. After a rest at these temperatures the withdrawal and boiling processes are repeated, the returned portion raising the temperature to 145–155° F. A third portion is then withdrawn and returned to give a final temperature of between 167–170° F.

In the Lautermaisch method the grist is placed on the false bottom of the mash tun and the liquor flooded in from the bottom at a temperature of about 176° F. This floats the goods off the false bottom, allowing the liquor to penetrate through. Thirty minutes later agitation or stirring is commenced and this too proceeds for thirty minutes. After a short rest to allow the goods to settle the thick wort is drawn off and transferred to the lauter tun, where it is boiled for about 75 minutes. This is then returned to the mash tun, some going under and some over the goods. A second mash is begun, again a short rest before the wort is drawn off. Sparging can then begin.

In passing, a preserving pan with lid makes an ideal lauter tun.

Here is a modification to this form of mashing: After the ground malt has been placed in the tun, sufficient liquor is added to moisten it, the liquor temperature being about 122° F. The soaking lasts for an hour, after which hotter liquor is added to raise the mash temperature to 132° F. At this point the goods are agitated or stirred for thirty minutes. They are then left to settle prior to drawing off the wort. This is boiled and returned to the tun, bringing the temperature up to 160° F. Mashing is recommenced for a further 45 minutes and the wort drawn off. Either of these methods will ensure a larger dextrin to maltose ratio.

The Dickmaisch process differs from the previous two examples as follows. After the ground malt has been placed in the tun, cold water is added and after a thorough mixing the resultant mash is allowed to stand for an hour. After this time hot liquor is entered, under and over the goods, and the temperature raised to 100° F whilst agitation or stirring takes place, the proportion of malt to liquor being about 2½ lb. to the gallon. As soon as the temperature becomes stable a quarter of the entire mash, including the goods, is drawn off and boiled for 30 minutes after which the wort is strained off and the goods returned to the tun, which raises the mash temperature to about 125° F. Mashing is recommenced and again a quarter of the entire mash is drawn off and boiled for 30 minutes, the goods strained off and the wort returned to the tun. This should now bring the temperature up to 140–145° F. After a resting period the wort is drawn off. Sparging is then commenced.

One can see how important it is to keep records. A good record or reference book is worth its weight in gold, being the story of high success and occasional dismal failure, by studying it regularly you should eventually be able to emulate the former regularly and eliminate the latter.

CHAPTER IX

Boiling and Cooling

Immediately the run off of the wort is completed the hops are added and boiling commences as quickly as possible. There are several reasons for this operation, and I find that most amateurs do not understand, or attach too little importance to, both the boiling and cooling of the wort.

Boiling ensures the full extraction of the flavours of the hops, not only adding to the pleasant character of the wort but assisting its stability. Portions of the albumin coagulate, and more and more precipitate as the temperature rises. Some of the more soluble portions in the mash are unaffected by the temperatures, but when boiling commences they assume solid form (just as, indeed, does the white of an egg). The operation also has the important factor of sterilising the must, helped by the antiseptics released from the hops.

The length of the boil is extremely important. Most brewers agree that a short period of boiling is not to be recommended. Boiling for a quarter or half an hour is insufficient to coagulate most of the albumin, or to extract the preservative values and flavours of the hops. The duration of the boil should be between one and a half to three hours, and most brewers settle for a standard two hours. One should allow a fierce boil to get a good coagulation, remembering that up to seven per cent per hour of the wort will be lost through evaporation if an open container is used. This will result in the wort becoming concentrated. This loss should be adjusted. There is also an increase in colour, which, it is thought is due to an oxidation of the dissolved substances. However too much notice should not be taken of this fact, for some part of this colour is lost during the fermentation.

It has long been accepted that there is a loss of hop fragrance during the boiling period. It is a common practice to hold back a percentage of the total of the hops and add them during the latter part of the boil in order to restore this loss. How efficient this is is open to conjecture, suffice it to say that one school of thought believes that dry hopping yields better results. So it is a case of "Yer pays yer price an' takes yer pick". I suggest you try both methods. Other changes take place during the boiling, such as the release of tannins from the hops; this dry astringency may add something to the taste of the finished beer. We have the salt reactions between the organic and inorganic calcium and phosphate which brings the pH down a little.

As soon as the boiling is finished the cooling is commenced by running the wort and hops through a wortbag, filter, or strainer. The hops assist by also acting as a filter as the wort runs through them. I cannot emphasise too strongly the importance of having a RAPID cooling of the wort to a temperature of 58–59° F. You may have problems in achieving this, but the following suggestions may be of help. An old refrigerator with the shelves removed will take a five gallon container. This can also be used for lager production. Polythene bags packed with ice, are useful, or clear plastic tubing coiled up the inside of the container. Cold water is circulated through the coils, and the outlet drained off. A cold, shaded concrete floor helps and in very cold winter weather you can just put the container outside. These suggestions may give you other ideas but whatever method you use make sure that it becomes a permanent part of your brewing practise. Keep 58–59° F imprinted on your mind.

It is essential for optimum yeast growth to have oxygen in the now cold wort. Lack of oxygen will result in a slower fermentation which could have dire results. The following information illustrates the importance of rapid cooling. Some brewers drop their temperatures from 150 to 60° F in 8 to 9 seconds, others find a slower cooling of 30 seconds to be suitable for their needs. All these temperatures and timings are relevant to infusion mashings. Decoction mashing follows the same strict rulings but with one slight variation. Ideally a good lager wort should be dropped to 42–43° F and, as we shall see, fermented at that temperature.

The coagulation of the albumin during boiling and the consequent clarification is called the hot break. A similar action takes place during the cooling, for as this proceeds small particles can be observed in the wort. This is called the cold break or the fine break. These can be satisfactorily removed either by fining or by filtering.

CHAPTER X

The Use of The Hydrometer

Since the repealing of the old laws on brewing by the 1963 Chancellor, Reginald Maudling, the amateur is no longer tied down to making beer not exceeding a certain given strength.

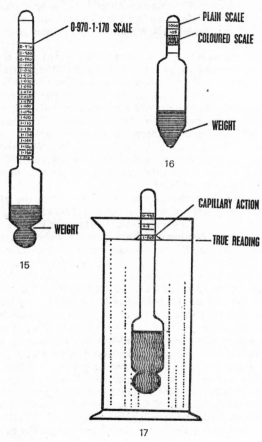

0·970-1·170 SCALE

PLAIN SCALE

COLOURED SCALE

WEIGHT

16

WEIGHT

15

CAPILLARY ACTION

TRUE READING

17

He can range over many gravities, but I confess to certain misgivings when someone says that they have a beer "as strong as whisky". After all, we have an instrument that can be of invaluable help in controlling the gravities to produce the different beers we want, and that instrument is the Hydrometer. It will give us the exact gravity readings of the brews before, during, and after fermentation, and by a simple piece of arithmetic we can also discover the alcoholic strength of the brews we have made. In a word, the hydrometer gives us— CONTROL.

Whilst appearing to be a complicated instrument it is in reality very simple to use. It is a slim glass tube with a bulb and balance weight at its base, (see sketches 15 to 17). The slim portion carries a scale. Scales vary, but the one suitable for wine and beer makers has a reading of 0.980° to 1.170° In sketch 16 we have a "bottling hydrometer", which is a "sawn off" version of the more conventional type. It consists of three readings, i.e. 1.010, 1.005, and 1.000. The first two readings and graduations are coloured showing when NOT to bottle, whilst the 1.003–1.000 readings are in white, implying the "safe" reading to bottle.

How does the conventional type work? Well the gravity (and mark this well) of water at 59° F is 1.000 S.G. (Specific Gravity). Therefore if we place our hydrometer in plain water we should see a reading of 1.000 where the water cuts across the scale. Care should be exercised when taking the reading because owing to capillary action the liquid will ride up the stem, thus giving a false reading, as we see in sketch 17. Look through the trial jar and take the reading on a line straight through the surface of the liquid. If we pitch into the trial jar sugar and malt extract and blend it with the water the resultant liquor will be "thicker", so our hydrometer when placed in this will be more buoyant and will ride higher than in the plain water. A simple and useful proof is to take a pint of water, which we know has a specific gravity of 1.000. Add two pounds of sugar to the water and dissolve. When cold, take the gravity and you will find that the hydrometer will give no reading because of the density of the liquid. Another higher range hydrometer will give a reading of 300°. To sum up: the more dense the liquid, the higher the gravity reading.

Prior to pitching on our yeast, the wort has a density made up of malt, sugars etc., and the hydrometer reading obtained will be the starting gravity.

It is commonsense then, that to obtain a lower gravity we must get rid of those malts and sugars by some means. Fermentation provides the answer. The yeast attacks the sugars and malts and creates the alcohol required. Since alcohol is lighter than water we shall see our hydrometer sinking deeper into the liquid, getting nearer to 1.000 as the fermentation draws to its close. The alcoholic content of a brew is determined by subtracting the starting gravity from the closing gravity and dividing the answer by 7.36. For example, say we are making a bitter beer of pale ale standard and have adjusted the wort to a starting gravity of 1.046. At the completion of the fermentation, and before bottling, we find that the gravity has dropped to 1.000. So:

$$1.046 = \text{Starting Gravity}$$
$$1.000 = \text{Closing Gravity}$$

$$.046 = \text{By Subtraction}$$

Thus, 46 (drop in degrees) divided by 7.36 = $6\frac{1}{2}\%$ *alcoholic volume.*

As a guide to your own brewing requirements here are the recommended starting gravities of the various types of beers. Obviously you may care to vary these gravities to suit your own particular tastes.

1.030–1.035 Milds, Browns, Lights, some Bitters and Stouts, and Lager.

1.040–1.060 Best Bitters, Pale Ales, Strong Stouts, and Strong Lager.

1.070–1.100 Barley Wines and Strong Ales.

Very few commercial beers attain these gravities due to high production costs and the crippling duties levied. (Incidentally, when doing some research in a book published at the turn of the century I read that the starting gravity of a well known Irish stout was 1.072–1.073°; so maybe our own brews are not so heavy after all!) I remember well when I returned from abroad in 1938 my particular delight was to drop in at the "Jolly Farmer" on the junction of the Camberley, Aldershot road. Here I would purchase a pint of bitter, ten cigarettes, and a pork pie, and receive twopence change from a shilling. These two examples clearly show how times change, and not always for the better, But I deviate, albeit drooling at the thought.

When you have purchased your hydrometer and test jar it is a good thing to test it to ensure that the readings are correct. Fill the test jar with water and obtain a temperature of 59° F and the reading on the scale should be 1.000. Temperature variations will affect the scale readings and it becomes necessary to adjust them slightly to give correct readings.

Temperature Correction Table

To assist the student in obtaining the correct gravity readings due to fluctuating temperatures, here is a table giving varying temperatures and the degrees needed for the gravity correction.

Temperature in degrees F	Gravity Correction	Specific Gravity Correction
50	−1	−0.001
59	NIL (Correct)	NIL (Correct)
68	+1	+0.001
77	+2	+0.002
86	+3	+0.003
95	+5	+0.005

When taking a reading make sure that the hydrometer is completely immersed into the liquid then let it find its own level. Semi-solid particles in the form of yeast etc. should not be allowed to adhere to the instrument. It must be remembered that at the outset of the fermentation the heavy carbon dioxide gas will "lift" the hydrometer thus giving a false reading, but at the crucial time for bottling this gas will be largely dormant, so a correct reading should be obtained. Should it be necessary to get an accurate reading at the early stages of the fermentation the sample should be drawn off into the test jar and thoroughly agitated by means of a swizzle stick or similar device. This will drive off most of the gas and give a more accurate reading. One should constantly bear in mind that many beers, particularly the heavy varieties such as barley wine have a high reading due to the unfermentable solids in them. Vigilance is essential to note when the fermentation is petering out despite the high reading on the scale. I conducted an experiment on some fifteen commercial barley wines and discovered that the lowest residual gravity was 5° and the highest 23°! The average was 19°! These figures should prove the importance of constant checking.

CHAPTER XI

Fermentation

Fermentation can occur at all temperatures between 32° and 131° F, but the most favourable are those from 59–68° F. The exception to this rule is, of course, lager, which enjoys a much lower temperature. It is therefore essential to create the correct conditions to carry out the fermentation. Thought must be given to the type of beverage being produced, and then will come the formulation of yeast type or types, temperatures to be employed, and so on.

Pasteur points out that the temperature at which a fermentation is carried out has a distinct influence on the flavour of the beer produced. Another important factor to creating these conditions, as we have seen in the chapter on Mashing and Cooling, is the necessity to cool the wort rapidly.

The following are the suggested temperatures for the main beers we produce.

Pale Ales should be fermented at 57–58° F.

Mild Ales should be fermented at 60–61° F.

Stout and Porter should be fermented at 64–65° F.

Lager should be fermented at 42–50° F. (max).

These temperatures are the pitching temperatures which will rise as the fermentation proceeds. It is advisable to try to hold down the temperature to as near as the pitching temperature as possible.

It is important that a thoroughly active yeast—be it high or low, is ready for pitching on to the wort as soon as it cools to these temperatures. The amateur should keep a careful check on temperatures throughout the fermentation. As the yeast multiplies so will the fermentation become more turbulent, create heat, and raise the wort's temperature slightly. We can resort to the cooling methods suggested in the chapter on Mashing and Cooling to hold the heat to the prescribed levels.

It is a good thing to filter the wort prior to fermenting for it gives a good aeration and will make for healthy yeast development, It is said that yeast from a filtered wort is firmer and activates quicker than that from unfiltered wort. But a word of warning on the pitfalls of over-aeration. Wort exposed to air is a natural target for air borne bacteria and disease ferments. Let us summarise the important lessons learnt between the cooling of the wort and the subsequent fermentation. Slow cooling of the wort can produce oxidation of the hop constituents which will reduce both the aroma and flavour of the beer.

The ideal fermentation can therefore be summed up as follows. Rapid cooling and filtration of the wort. The pitching of a thoroughly activated yeast. The protection from exposure to the air, and regulated temperature control.

The fermenting vessels in some modern breweries are completely enclosed and the CO_2 generated is drawn off and collected via pressure lines. I have applied this technique—quite successfully—using a stainless steel enclosed tank and fitting a relief valve, set to open at 6–8 p.s.i., the gas, of cours escaping to atmosphere. The fermenting wort was carefully transferred over to the enclosed vessel after the skimming operation had been completed. One advantage of the enclosed fermentation vessel, providing the skimming operation has been hygienically successful, is that in the enclosed vessel a barrier of CO_2 is created above the fermenting wort. This is an ideal deterrent to bacterial infection.

After pitching the activated yeast on to the wort we shall see bubbles rising to the surface after about three hours, indicating the commencement of the fermentation. After a further three hours a slight froth will appear which gradually spreads to cover the whole of the wort surface in the fermenting vessel. It is at this point that temperature control of the wort is put in hand for if left unchecked the temperature could rise to as high as 90° F. The yeast head continues to grow and takes the form known as the "cauliflower head". Latterly this turns to a rocky surface. Skimming of the excess yeast should be thorough and at three to four hour intervals. Care must be taken to ensure that the wort is kept away from the ring of yeast which collects round the periphery of the fermenting vessel. Failure to do this could result in a yeast bitten beer. This can be done simply by drawing off some of the wort until the bulk is well below the yeast mark. Then, with a clean, damp cloth wipe away the yeast until the vessel is thoroughly clean. Lastly, replace the wort drawn off.

Hydrometer checks will be taken throughout the fermentation as to how attenuation is proceeding. Before this is completed it must be decided what kind of priming will be employed, if priming is to be resorted to. The brewer may decide to barrel or bottle when the hydrometer reading is about 1.006° and so avoid the priming operation. The alternatives are priming with syrup, or "Krausening", the latter being when a thoroughly active wort is added to the attenuated beer in the ratio of two pints of active wort to five gallons. All three methods will give a secondary fermentation.

CHAPTER XII

Draught Beer Production

The amateur can produce draught beers quite easily but he must not expect to obtain the type of beers that are produced in bottle. As has been said draught beers have a totally different character from bottled beers. Having established this, let us see how draught beer is produced. Obviously we shall need a barrel of the traditional oak type or the more modern stainless steel or alloy variety. It would be as well to define the sizes here.

A PIN: 4½ Gallons.

A FIRKIN: 9 Gallons.

A KILDERKIN or KILN: 18 Gallons.

A BARREL: 36 Gallons.

A HOGSHEAD: 54 Gallons.

The recommended size for the student should be a Pin. On obtaining a barrel it should be thoroughly inspected before being taken into use. The ends and shives should be free from cracks and completely watertight. Perhaps the barrel has not been used for some time and will leak due to its having dried out, but if it is in good condition the wood will swell when wet, thus closing the joints. The bung holes should be undamaged and capable of receiving bungs to make a gas-tight joint. The barrel should be steamed before use. After steaming it is a good thing to "sniff" inside the barrel. The nose should soon detect any trace of sour beer, barrel stink, acetification, or any other impurity. After this operation, if all is well, swill the barrel round with a solution of sodium metabisulphite or a strong solution of Campden tablets, and this will eliminate most bacteria. Suitable bungs and spiles should be available, and of course a serving tap. Bungs are the discs of hardwood which are flogged into the bunghole and taphole to seal off the cask after filling. The taphole bung is the smaller of the two and has a grooved ring running within the diameter. When broaching a cask the tap is placed in the centre of this grooved ring and hit smartly with a mallet. This knocks the disc into the cask and the tap firmly into the bung. Make sure that the tap, if a wooden one, is soaked in clean water for some hours before use. The filler bung is slightly tapered and this too has a grooved ring of roughly $\frac{3}{8}''$ diameter; this is to receive the spile or peg, a round, tapered piece of either hardwood or softwood. The hardwood spile is used to seal off the barrel, leaving no gas escape. The softwood spile, on the other hand, is porous and will allow seepage of excess gas pressure. After ensuring that all these are covered we find ourselves ready for racking the beer into the barrel. The barrel is filled with the beer, after emptying the metabisulphite solution, then primed with sugar, sugar syrup, or a commercial primer. As a guide to quantity make a solution of syrup using two pounds of sugar to one pint of water. Six fluid ounces of this syrup to $4\frac{1}{2}$ gallons should be used as a primer. A little air space should be left at the top of the barrel to allow for gas expansion during maturation, thus avoiding the chance of a bung being blown out. Before sealing off the cask finings may be added. These are covered in the chapter on Fining and Filtration.

Having fined the beer, there is one more operation that can be undertaken before sealing down the barrel. This is a practice called "dry hopping" resorted to by some breweries. All that is involved is the addition of a small amount of hops to each barrel before sealing down. The modern practice is to use "hop pellets". These, as the name implies, are circular pellets of compressed hops, weighing approximately half an ounce. Since dry hopping involves getting them into the barrel via the narrow aperture of the bunghole the advantages of using pellets can be readily seen. Having completed this operation, if decided upon, the barrel is sealed down to allow the beer to mature and for the hops to convey that little extra piquancy to the brew. It is essential for the barrel to be cradled and chocked on to some form of gantry. At no time should the cask be left lying on its staves. After leaving for the necessary maturation period the cask can be tapped and spiled. Since this can cause some disturbing of the lees it is necessary to do this at least 24 hours before the beer is needed for serving.

Once open, the cask should be emptied as soon as possible, and if you have made your brew correctly this should not be a difficult task—particularly at party time! The longer you have the beer after tapping the cask, and the more beer emptied from it, the more gas expended, and so it will be necessary to restore this loss of gas pressure. This is done by repriming the remainder of the beer, and hard spiling the cask to make it gas tight. Raising the temperature round the barrel will assist the quicker restoration of gas pressure. Check before serving. Finally, as the cask is emptied it should be chocked up gradually from the rear. This is "putting the barrel on the tilt" and it is done to allow the beer to flow more readily, but mainly to avoid the lees being disturbed so as not to cloud the remaining beer. After we have sadly removed the last remnants of the brew the barrel must be thoroughly cleansed and steamed. Then fill it with clean water containing Campden or metabisulphite solution until required for the next brew. Barrels should never be left to dry out for any great length of time. The shrinkage could cause the hoops to slip and then it becomes a job for that—alas, now diminishing class of craftsman—the cooper, provided that there is one left in your area. Some breweries retain the odd cooper who pursues his fine craft in different guise, making highly polished half barrels for shrubs and plants and there is one brewery which does a lively trade exporting them. So try your local brewery for any repairs that you may require. If they have no coopers they may be able to advise you of a brewery which has.

In sketch 18 we see a sectioned barrel on the tilt which contained a naturally conditioned deposit beer. Let us now turn our attention to the modern trend in brewing, the carbonated or keg beer. This is a beer which has had all the yeast removed by filtering. The sparkle is put back into the beer by the injection of CO_2 gas. This, of course, has to be regulated and a pressure of 6 to 12 p.s.i. is recommended. The student can produce this type of beer in two ways as we see in sketches 19 and 21. Of the two I term the method shown in sketch 19 as the "professional" approach, whilst I call sketch 21 "the means to an end" method. Let us study sketch 19. The thoroughly filtered beer is racked into the barrel, leaving the normal air space. The bung houses the gassing tube which in turn is coupled to a non-return valve. A high pressure hose connects the inlet side of the non return valve to a CO_2 cylinder of the five or fourteen pounds size. Also housed in the bung is the pressure gauge and tube. Pressure gauges vary in their calibrations, but I have one which gives a range of from

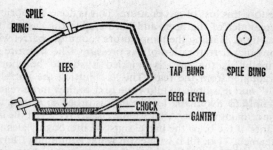

SPILE
BUNG

LEES

BEER LEVEL

CHOCK

GANTRY

TAP BUNG

SPILE BUNG

18. BARREL OF NATURALLY CONDITIONED DEPOSIT BEER ON THE TILT

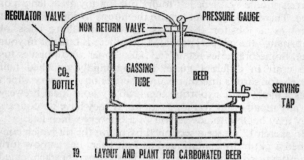

REGULATOR VALVE

NON RETURN VALVE

PRESSURE GAUGE

CO₂ BOTTLE

GASSING TUBE

BEER

SERVING TAP

19. LAYOUT AND PLANT FOR CARBONATED BEER

PUMP

BALLOON

FILLER LEVEL

3 gals.

BEER

DISPENSER

CARTRIDGE

20. USE OF AIR FOR PRESSURISING

21. CARBONATING WITH CO₂ CARTRIDGE

0–30 lb. p.s.i. in graduations of 1 lb. p.s.i. and I find this easy to read quickly and ideal for the job. Should you buy a second-hand gauge make sure that you have it checked before taking it into use.

With the beer in the cask, we insert the bung and open up *slowly* the regulator valve. Check the pressure gauge and when it reaches about 5 lb. p.s.i. hold it at this pressure whilst you check for any leak with soapy water brushed round the bung, the non return valve, the pressure gauge insert, and finally the hose connections between the non-return valve and the CO_2 bottle. Another method of finding a leak is to watch the pressure gauge. If it is seen that the needle is falling it can be assumed that there is a leak in the circuit. With the soapy water method bubbles will be seen where the leak occurs. With the circuit gas tight draw off a glass of the beer and check it for condition. If it is lacking in head retention increase the gas pressure until it meets your requirements. Should you require a further safety factor you can add a relief valve to the circuit. This can be set so that if it pressurises above the amount required the valve opens and drains off the excess gas.

If you have no wish to serve direct from the barrel, purchase a dispenser and a length of dairy quality polythene tube. The dispenser is clamped to the table or bar top and the polythene tubing connects the barrel to the dispenser.

In sketch 21 we have a two gallon container of rigid, dairy quality plastic. In the screw-on lid is inserted a cartridge dispenser. All one has to do is insert a CO_2 cartridge and rotate the dispenser. The cartridge is pierced and the gas floods into the beer.

A recent addition to the brewing scene is an ingeniously-thought-out method and one which I thoroughly recommend. We know that in dispensing beer we gradually use up the gas—most of it in transferring the beer from container to glass. We also know that air should not come into contact with beer. In this method the bright beer is put into the keg to a maximum of three gallons, and priming sugar and finings (if required) are added. After a few days of secondary fermentation bubbles will be seen escaping through the water of a bubble chamber situated in the lid of the keg. When the bubbles cease it indicates the end of the secondary fermentation and when the beer reaches maturity it can be dispensed. As the beer is used a ballon *inside* the keg and attached to a non-return valve is inflated via a pump, thus cleverly pressurising the keg without letting air get into contact with the beer. Incidentally the pump is capable of being disconnected for use on other kegs. The whole is well made, easy to clean, and simplicity itself to use.

CHAPTER XIII

Fining and Filtration

Let it be said at the outset that *bottled* beer should neither be fined nor filtered. Beer intended for bottling can be fined in bulk, prior to bottling. Similarly filtering in bulk can take place, after which a small amount of active yeast should be added to provide the secondary fermentation required in bottle.

First, finings which are really clarifying agents used mainly to remove particles of matter from suspension and thus render the finished beer, or wine polished or star bright.

It is only fair to say that some matters which affect a beer, such as wild yeasts, are unaffected by fining, but happily these are in a minority. How does fining work ? There was a popular misconception up until some years ago that finings spread over the surface of the liquid needing clarifying and gradually forced the particles out of suspension through sheer weight. This theory was completely disproved when a team of scientists discovered their true action.

Mr. John Mitchell in his lecture on "Finings" at the Middlesex Winemakers Festival summarised this action.

The colloids which give a wine or beer a turbid appearance are submicroscopic particles and the pH of the wine or beer contains a small electric charge of either positive or negative value to them. The charge is the same to all particles, and like charges repel each other, the particles staying in solution, each separate from its neighbour.

But if a fining is selected which, when it is made into a solution, will have the opposite charge to that present on the colloid of the wine or beer, when added, the charges will cancel each other out, and the neutral enlarged particles will no longer repel each other, so that deposition will take place.

It can be seen from this summary that there is a case for fining before filtration. However one must be careful not to overfine as this could produce a haze. This hazard can be easily overcome if a test is carried out prior to making the main fining.

There are many types of finings used in clarifying beers and wines and it may be as well if we named them to familiarise ourselves as to their uses. Some would only be used in wine fining and those sympathetic to beer finings will be highlighted.

Gelatine. If using this medium ensure that the best quality is obtained. It should be dissolved in water, either warm or hot, but not boiling water. Mainly used as a wine fining.

White of Egg. (Albuminous Fining). The white of a fresh egg is whipped into a stiff froth before being used.

Ox Blood. This is another albuminous fining not greatly used today. These two finings are mainly used in red wines.

Casein. Fairly expensive. Used mainly in white wines.

Bentonite. The American counterpart to Spanish Earth. It has the appearance of a white clay powder and is useful as a second fining.

Agar Agar. Produced from seaweed and is a colloidal fining.

Caragheen Moss. (Sometimes called Irish Moss). A product of Ireland and a fining used in brewing. It is a copper fining, that is to say it is added to the wort at the boiling stage.

Isinglass. Probably the principal fining agent used in brewing. It is the *purified* gelatin obtained from part of the gut of the sturgeon. It is a simple matter to make up one's own finings as follows. Put into a sterilised bottle ½ pint of warm water, add isinglass, (about the size of a walnut). Since we must have a cutting agent add a teaspoonful of tartaric acid and finally half a Campden tablet. Shake thoroughly and place into a warm place such as an airing cupboard. Shake periodically and after about two days the isinglass will have dissolved and the whole will be a gelatinous mass. These finings are then added to the beer, using roughly 4–5 oz. to the 4½ gallons (Pin). Never make up more finings than you will need for your immediate requirements.

Again I must emphasise the advisability of running tests on some of the beer prior to using the finings on the full batch. Remember, overfining can *cause* hazes.

For those who wish to complete their knowledge of finings commercial types can be tried. These can be obtained from brewers suppliers, the addresses of which can be obtained from the trade journals such as "The Brewers Guardian" or "The Brewers Journal".

We now come to filtration. A dictionary definition runs thus: "FILTER. Cloth or other apparatus for straining liquids, pass, flow through, leak out, percolate." Filtering Press.—Apparatus for extracting oil from fish! (I do not think that this one is relevant!) Filter Pump—apparatus for expediting filtration. Centrifuge.

Basically the difference between Fining and Filtration can be defined as: Fining takes place in the container, whilst filtration occurs after leaving the container en route to another container.

Filtration can be done on a gravity basis, or as the dictionary defines, by a filter pump. This is a mechanical pump which speeds up the filtration process.

There are many filtration media:

Filter Pulp. Is usually made up of cotton fibres with a percentage of asbestos pulp added. It must be emphasised that the pulp should be thoroughly washed prior to being used or a pulp flavour could contaminate the beer.

Filter Cloths and Filter Papers. These can be used but remember to ensure that the correct grade is obtained since these are capable of giving from coarse to fine filtering results. Cloths and papers, like pulp, should be thoroughly washed.

"Jelly Bag". This is an old form of filtering. It is a canvas bag, sausage shaped, which is filled with filter pulp and attached to the stem of a funnel. The liquid to be filtered is poured into the funnel whence the colloids become enmeshed in the pulp, leaving the liquid to run bright.

Another method is filtration by vacuum. This is achieved by having a filter pump to create the vacuum. This is attached to the cold tap of the ordinary domestic water supply. The second requirement is a filter flask which has a broad base which tapers narrowly at the top. The pump and flask are joined together by a short piece of stout rubber sleeve which is placed over the glass tubes let into the walls of the pump and flask. Into the top of the flask is fitted a funnel containing the filter aid. Since this apparatus could be fairly costly it may be necessary to resort to one of the other methods. On the other hand once the principle of operation is understood it can be adapted, using alternate materials.

A modern method of filtration which is being used in increasing amounts is the use of KEISELGUHR (diatomaceous silica). It is claimed (Moll 1951) that for some beers this method of filtration gives better carbon dioxide retention, a more compact head, and a better hop flavour.

The student would do well to note carefully the phrase SOME BEERS. So many things are involved in filtration that a method suitable to one beer could be unsuitable to another. Over-filtration can cause the impairing of the foaming character of the beer and lead to colour removal, and, finally, if the pulp has not been efficiently washed, off tastes can develop.

CHAPTER XIV

Beer Types—Draught and Bottled

One subject which often puzzles the beginner is the make-up of the various types of beer, whether they be bottled or draught. It must be realised at the outset that there is little or no difference in the ingredients used in producing bottled and draught beers. A mild ale is the draught equivalent of a brown ale. Ordinary draught bitter becomes a light ale in its bottled form and best bitter is the draught equivalent of bottled pale ale. The difference emerges after the brew has been barrelled or bottled, matured and is poured. At this point comes the parting of the ways for the bottled beer will have a completely different characteristic from its draught counterpart. There are obviously exceptions to this rule; (a brewery will sometimes make a beer solely for bottling or draught purposes) but for economic reasons these are very few and far between.

Another thing which seems to cause some confusion is the colour of beer. A lot of nonsense is talked about all bitters having to be pale or light straw, or dark beers having to be brown ales. I recall my father trying a new bitter type at one of the Brewers Exhibitions. It was as green as Creme de Menthe and of excellent flavour, I wonder where this would fit in with the "Bar Expert's" grading? As we shall see, beers vary in colour according to the brewery, its locality and liquor. We know that Pilsen lager is light in colour, yet Munich lager is dark. The green bitter was, no doubt, a gimmick but it proves that beer has no set colour standards. Prior to their knowledge of water treatment brewers had to produce their beers from waters which might have a heavy chalk content or other mineral deposits. Pale coloured beers would have shown a haze or lack of star brightness, so the brews were coloured with caramel and other things to mask these deficiencies. It is a strange fact that whilst nearly all breweries employ modern water techniques many have to carry on producing the same coloured beers that they have always produced. Psychology demands it. Your average beer drinker is a person of fixed habits. He will stick to one brew, even to one brewery. Give him his normal drink but change the colour and he will give every excuse he can think of to prove that it is not his normal drink!

Having got these matters into perspective let us look at these many beer types, starting with draught and going on to the bottled varieties.

Draught Beers

Mild Ale. This is produced from pale and amber malts, and is lightly hopped. The starting gravity is approximately 1.030°.

Bitter. Produced with the use of pale malt and possibly additions of either flaked rice or maize. It is heavier hopped than mild ale.

Best Bitter. Uses pale malt and additional adjuncts. The hop content and the alcoholic content are higher than in ordinary bitter. The starting gravity is around 1.045°.

Stout. The Irish stout being served today is mostly from metal casks or kegs which has a gas cylinder within the cask. Here a gas mixture is transferred to the stout by means of non-return and regulator valves, the pressure within the keg being controlled by the latter. This ensures a good head to the stout. At this point it will be noted that nearly all modern beers are pasteurised then artificially impregnated with carbon dioxide gas. It is a heartening sign that one brewery is returning to producing the old cask matured beers, complete with beer engines and pumps. Long may they reign! And I hope that the other large combines follow suit.

Bottles Beers

Brown Ale. This type of beer varies tremendously throughout the country. The main characteristics are a smooth, slightly sweet, lightly hopped beverage. The bouquet should be rich and malty, and the alcoholic content light. Colour varies as to the locality but ranges from amber to deep brown.

Light Ale. Here we have a beer with a starting gravity of around 1.030°, so it will be light in alcohol. It should be smooth and refreshing to the palate and the bouquet should have a lightly hopped quality. The colour ideally should be straw, with a brilliant, polished appearance.

Pale Ale. Higher in starting gravity than light ale and therefore higher in alcohol. The hopping should be more pronounced than in light ale. Colours should range from straw to light amber.

India Pale Ale, Stingo, Export. These are beers of great strength with a starting gravity of around 1.045°. Originally brewed to stand storage whilst being shipped to far-off countries. Heavily hopped and robust in character, this is a beer to be respected when made by the amateur.

Sweet Stout. This was once known as "milk stout" due to the use of a non fermentable substance called lactose. This was used solely to attain the required sweetness without the risk of fermentation. The starting gravity, about 1.035°, results in a light alcoholic content. The residual gravity can be as high as 12. The water should be soft. The taste should be smooth with a fully rounded flavour, the acidity should be low and the hop content light. A pleasant malted flavour should be noted.

Irish type Stout. This is a dry, robust, pleasant drink of great character. The starting gravity should be approximately 1.045°, and therefore the alcoholic content will be high. The colour should be liquorice and the head deep oatmeal. The water should be soft. The bouquet should be a fully grained one, whilst the taste should be full bodied, extremely dry, with a slightly bitter and "iron-like" taste, due to the use of chocolate and black malts.

Barley Wine. These are the "vintage" beers of great body and character. With a starting gravity as high as 1.080–1.100° they are as individual as a gallery of old masters. Some will be straw coloured, others deep amber or walnut. One will be well hopped, another heavily malted, one will be dry to the palate, yet another will be sweet. One will be a straight brew, another will be a carefully calculated blend of beers. The two things that will be common to all is the high price, and that they will be served in "nips" or six ounce bottles. Maturing can take up to two years.

Lager. This is a beer that is not really understood by the rank and file of the drinking public, or even the amateur brewer, although the demand is increasing. It would be as well therefore if lager was studied at some length.

First let us examine the word "lager". This is simply the German word for "store", which indicates that we are dealing with a beer capable of being brewed and kept for long periods. With modern requirements for quick returns for laid out

87

capital this term should be treated with some caution for not all lagers are as heavy in gravity as in years gone by, indeed, some lagers being brewed today are weak. True lagers derive their characteristics from the flavours obtained from the slow fermentation methods employed, combined with the use of the yeast *sacch. carlsbergensis*. The high alcohol yield ensures long maturing and storage. Brewing is by the decoction system. There is little doubt that lager beers originated in Bavaria, probably in the 15th. century, and it would appear that the use of "low" or bottom working yeast was well understood in Munich.

The church, always to the forefront in matters on wine and beer, took a hand, for a monk by the name of Groll succeeded in smuggling some of the yeast from Munich to Pilsen in the 1840's and so the pale, now world-renowned Pilsen lager was born. The romantic story of this yeast and its association with lager did not end there for far away in Denmark a brewer in the Carlsberg Brewery, one J. Jacobsen, returned from Munich with a quantity of the yeast. We are told that he cooled the yeast at every coach stop by pouring water over the container. Students would do well to emulate the patience of this man, for the year was 1845, and the coach in which he travelled was drawn by a team of horses. The next step in the remarkable story came in 1883 when Emil Chris Hansen succeeded in isolating a pure yeast cell, and growing a culture which it was possible to pitch on to a small brew. Further research produced apparatus capable of producing a continuous production of pure yeast. In 1886 Hansen made known his intention of patenting the apparatus he had perfected but Jacobsen would not hear of it, declaring that the results of research from the Carlsberg Laboratories were open to the world, a decision that brewers the world over should acclaim.

Further differences between lager and English beers are in the hops and malt used. Lager hops are invariably of continental origin, and varieties such as Saaz, Hallertau, Spalt, and Styrian Goldings are used. Blends of hops are also favoured by some brewers. Lager hops are seedless and it is thought that these strains do not produce the drowsiness experienced by drinking beers which use the seeded varieties. The malt, too, is different from that used in English beers, in that it is lighter malted. Liquor used in Munich has a low concentration of sulphates and chlorides but a moderate concentration of salt. The liquor of Pilsen has low salt concentration and has a very soft texture. The starting gravity should be about 1.060°.

To sum up: Preferably use a light malt, the hops should be seedless, the yeast should be a bottom working variety, and the liquor should be soft and low in salt concentration. The decoction system should be used in the mashing. Finally, it is essential that the fermentation be conducted in cool temperatures ranging from 53° F to as low as 42° F. Keep the word "Lager" constantly before you and remember that the word store means slow maturing in bottle at cool temperatures. To produce this drink is a challenge to the amateur but it is one worth taking for experience gained will prove of inestimable value. It will be of interest to those living near to, or visiting Wrexham to learn that most of the public houses serve lager on draught as opposed to bitter beer. This is due to a number of German merchants who formed a syndicate and built a lager brewery at the end of the last century. They appear to have experienced great trouble for they were made bankrupt at the beginning of this century. Fortunately the brewery was restarted successfully so that today lager enjoys a better sale than bitter in this area, another proof that the public's drinking habits are very difficult to change.

Honey Beer. This brew must surely emanate from early history when honey was one of the well known sweeteners sometimes the only one, and mead was its fermented by-product. No doubt the ready availability and cheapness of sugar saw the decline and fall of this beer, although it still survives in Norfolk, thanks to a brewery in that area. It should be produced as a light coloured beer with a starting gravity of 1.045°. It is obvious that honey should be substituted for sugar. The type of honey to be used is of the utmost importance since strong flavoured honey will influence the finished beer, in some cases to the point of nausea. One type of honey to avoid at all costs is the Australian honey derived from the Eucalyptus flower. Whilst this product is enjoyed in its natural state it is completely the reverse as a fermentable honey. Fermentation brings out pungent, and acrid tastes which completely ruin any brew produced from it. Mead makers shy from it and beer makers would do well to follow suit. If this type of honey is borne in mind one can safely venture through the many types of honey with a reasonable degree of safety. English and Canadian clover honey, Spanish and Californian orange blossom honey are all suitable for beer, though the two aforementioned are probably the favourites. Since honey carries bacteria hostile to good fermentations it is necessary to bring it to the boil and simmer for a short period, during which any unwanted matter will be skimmed off. Naturally the student should try to brew all beers in his, or her search for experience. With honey beer it would be a wise course to adopt by making a single gallon at the outset, for fermented honey is not everyone's idea of a drink. If you like it the volume of the pilot brew can be increased for successive ones.

Spruce Beer. This beer is now a rarity, though not completely extinct. It survives in certain parts of Britain, notably the Midlands and around the Merseyside. Produced from oil of spruce it imparts a fresh, clean taste to the palate and is an excellent thirst quencher on hot, sunny days. Brewers used to use oil of spruce as an adjunct to their beers, solely to leave the palate clean and fresh, although with modern techniques it is doubtful if this practice still survives. This does not mean that one should ignore this commodity. Indeed far from it. It is recommended that oil of spruce should be used in its own right and as an adjunct to a bitter beer. In some parts spruce beer is blended with a bitter beer, very much as a stout is mixed with a bitter. In Canada and the United States, the real home of the spruce, this type of beer should really gain popularity but wherever you are, make it and try it.

Birch Beer. This type is another very old form of beer making, and no doubt takes its roots from the time when the grain used in brewing was taxed and so the poor had to resort to other and more ingenious forms of producing a beverage capable of producing the same effects and tastes of beer. For the benefit of the more academically minded an old, original recipe is appended in the chapter dealing with basic recipes.

Herb Beers. Again Britain was probably responsible for the formation of herb beers due to the reasons mentioned in the last paragraph. On the other hand herbalists could have been responsible, since they are dedicated to their craft. Like Spruce and Birch beers, Herb beers are not recognised as true beers, but it is felt that their inclusion will be of interest to brewers the world over, so in the chapter dealing with basic recipes there are recipes for producing Nettle, Ginger, and other beers. With modern tendencies and the march of science it is not inconceivable that in time the modern brewer will not bother with ingredients, but will put a coin in a slot and receive a polythene bag marked with the types of beer mentioned in this chapter. After due constitution with aqua pura he will cook it on his micro-wave cooker, place it in a special container, ferment it out, allowing the impurities and yeast to be drawn off, and after artificially impregnating it with CO_2, serve to his guests. Isn't it a revolting thought? Let us therefore, at all times, keep to our traditional methods of brewing before us and ignore like the plague all ersatz forms of brewing.

CHAPTER XV

Conditioning Beer

Bringing beers into true conditions is of the utmost importance, and will only be achieved by knowledge and experience. Heat, cold, draught, humidity, gravity are amongst some of the things to be taken into consideration. It must be admitted that amateurs generally used to produce beers of too high a gravity, and drank them far too early. Today, however, most brewers realise these mistakes and in consequence are using lower gravities. Even so, their beers are still relatively strong and must be given time to attain maturity, and it would be as well if we understood the natural progression of beer during maturation. Our bottled beers, as we well know, are racked bottled, primed and sealed. Then follows a period of "sickness in bottle". In other words the small yeast residue in the bottle commences to work on the sugars, or priming agent and creates the carbon dioxide gas necessary for the required sparkle and head. This causes temporary instability in the beer and only time and good cellarmanship will rectify these conditions. It will be appreciated, too, that the beer is undergoing radical structural changes. As the days pass, the rough harshness found in the new beer will begin to dissipate, and a rounder, smoother, and fuller flavoured taste will manifest itself.

Thus we now see why a light beer with, say a starting gravity of 1.035° conditions and matures much more quickly than a barley wine where the starting gravity is around 1.080°. We know that temperature stability must be attained and the following should prove to be of interest and amply illustrate this point. I recall that our bottling stores were very heavily blanketed at the doors, whilst in the centre of the floor stood a gas ring with a fire brick on top. This rather primitive device gave a static temperature of 58° F, and hundreds of dozens of beers lay around the walls gently maturing. Then after some six weeks, with a firm yeast deposit, and a star bright condition they were dispatched to quench some parched throat. In those days these beers would have a starting gravity of 1.055°–60°. No doubt the modern brewer reading this form of maturing would throw up his arms in horror, when thinking of the modern methods at his disposal. However at the period in question we had just finished a long and bloody war, and the blankets were war-surplus horse blankets and thermostatic controls, air conditioning, and other sophisticated improvements were things of the future. Since necessity is the mother of invention that old gas ring and brick did as much as any streamlined modern console.

You may be at some disadvantage with regards to attaining the ideal conditions, but as we have already proved, with a little ingenuity you should be able to achieve your aims. Therefore on hot, sunny days when the beer is likely to "fret" the following hints may be of use. A zinc bath full of cold water, or the water butt in your garden—providing that it is in a sheltered position, will make ideal receptacles for cooling beer. A concrete floor is worth considering, but if warm or hot air is circulating, a damp sack placed over the bottles will ensure that a cool current of air flows round them. A barrel can be treated in like manner. Tie two bricks together with string so that they hang halfway down the barrel with a third lying on top. Have this contraption at each end of the barrel and place a wet sack over the bricks. The air on the inside of the sack will be cool. It may be necessary to use a soft spile (see chapter on draught beer) in these conditions to take off surplus gas pressure. Whatever you do, do not *store* your beer in a refrigerator. One sees in modern bars these days large trays containing beers which are chilled, and *not refrigerated*. So on hot days place your immediate requirements in the refrigerator and *lightly* chill before serving. Beers which are over chilled will lose their delicate bouquets, tastes and flavours and will become dull to the palate.

In very cold weather it may be necessary to resort to artificial means to attain the necessary degree of heat required for maturing purposes. An old cupboard, shelved to take the bottles, and heated by a 20 Watt lamp. A small paraffin heater, as used for car sumps will burn for about a week without requiring attention. A night light placed under a slightly raised plant pot. A cupboard built over hot water pipes. A tea chest housing a 20 watt lamp. All these ideas will illustrate the simplicity with which cold can be overcome. It may be that a cold snap descends on our matured beers and so starves them. Since these beers would be dull and uninteresting to the taste we must bring our immediate requirements forward and if time permits, place them before the fire or some form of heater for a period of time. If these items are not available put the The Happy Brewer—Gal. 23—Folio 56—9/10 times—20 ems bottles into a bowl or zinc bath of warm water. Change the water from time to time to ensure continual warmth. Again care must be taken to safeguard against overheating.

CHAPTER XVI

Basic Recipes

Having digested the many theoretical sides of brewing let us proceed to put this knowledge into practical use. The following recipes are intended to cover the many types of beer we drink—but remember they are only *basic* recipes. In other words they are intended to form the springboard from which you may dive into formulating beers modified to suit your palate and those of your friends.

Your friends are a very important part of your brewing experience, for their constructive criticism is invaluable to your formulations and besides, nothing fills you with greater pleasure than to see the look of ecstasy on their faces as they partake of your latest masterpiece! In the chapter on beer types we found that over the centuries many types of beers have been drunk and enjoyed so let these ancient beverages have an airing. Who knows, you may be pleasantly surprised at the recipes of our ancestors?

LIGHT ALE (hard water)

Definition. *A beer with a starting gravity of 1.030°–1.035°, and in consequence light in alcohol. The bouquet should be lightly hopped. The taste will have a balance of hops and grain. The colour should be that of straw, the condition brilliant with a good head retention.*

Recipe for 5 gallons

6¼ lb. pale malt	1¼ lb. wheat syrup
3¾ oz. golding hops	10 oz. crystal malt
Yeast	Sugar to 1.030° (if required)

Add the crushed grains and wheat syrup to about 2½ gallons of water and mash at a temperature of 146–150° F, until the starch end-point is reached (iodine test). Drain off liquor and sparge with water which is 170° F. Check gravity and if under 1.030° add sugar syrup until this figure is reached. Add hops and boil in a closed container for 45 minutes. Cool rapidly by adding cold water until the 5 gallon mark is reached. Pitch yeast and try to hold the fermentation down to 58° F. Bottle and open when 4 to 6 weeks old. The same procedure for draught.

INDIA PALE ALE OR BEST BITTER (hard water)

Definition. *This beer is the most popular brewed. The starting gravity should be 1.045° so the alcoholic content will be fairly high. The bouquet should be redolent of hops and grain. This hop and grain content should come out well on the taste, together with its cleanness and freshness. A good head retention should be sought.*

Recipe for 5 gallons (hard water)

2¼ lb. pale malt   10 oz. flaked rice
8 oz. flaked wheat   15 oz. crystal malt
2 lb. D.M.S. malt extract   3 oz. styrian hops
Cane invert sugar to 1.045°   2 oz. golding hops
Caragheen (Irish) moss

Bring water up to 150° F, and add crushed grains and malt extract and mash at this temperature until the starch end-point is reached. Add sugar as syrup, hops, and prepared Caragheen Moss and boil for 45 minutes. Run off and sparge with liquor at 170° F. Bring up to 5 gallon volume. Cool rapidly and pitch yeast. Hold ferment to 58° F. Bottle and open when 6 to 8 weeks old. The same procedure for draught.

BROWN ALE (fairly soft water)

Definition. *This beer has a variety of tastes ranging from the very sweet London brown ales to the amber coloured, drier Newcastle Brown Ale. The starting gravity is 35°, and the residual gravity should be around 5–7°, and an alcoholic content of 3%. Other characteristics are a good head, oatmeal in colour, and a lively working bead.*

Recipe for 5 gallons

4 lb. pale malt   10 oz. crystal malt
10 oz. wheat syrup   10 oz. porage oats
2½ oz. fuggles hops   Liquid Sweetex to taste
Demerara sugar to S.G. 1.035°   Top fermenting yeast
Caragheen (Irish) moss

Mash grains, wheat syrup, porage oats at 138° F, until starch end point is reached. Adjust gravity with Demerara sugar, add hops and Caragheen Moss and simmer for 30 minutes. Cool rapidly and add yeast. Ferment out and adjust sweetness with Sweetex. Bottle and serve when 4 to 6 weeks old.

DRY AND SWEET STOUT (fairly soft water)

Definition. *Sweet stout was once known as "Milk Stout" through the use of lactose to attain the necessary sweetness. Starting gravity is 1.035°, and the residual gravity can be as high as 12°. The taste should be smooth with a pleasant, malted flavour, lightly hopped and low acidity.*

Dry stout is robust, with great character. The starting gravity should be around 1.045° yielding an alcoholic content of 5%. The bouquet should be fully grained, with a full bodied taste, extremely dry and "iron like".

SWEET STOUT. Recipe for 5 gallons

3½ lb. pale malt	½ lb. Lamberts silicose caramel
6 oz. crystal malt	8 oz. porage oats
Demerara sugar to 1.035°	Guinness yeast
3½ oz. Whitbread golding hops	Liquid sweetex

Add crushed malts and oats to liquor and mash at 138° F. When starch free run off wort and boil with hops and silcose for 35 minutes. Adjust gravity with sugar syrup to 1.035°. Cool rapidly, add active yeast and ferment out at 60° F. Taste prior to bottling and adjust sweetness with Sweetex. (4 drops equals one teaspoonful of sugar). Bottle and prime in the normal manner. Serve after 4 to 6 weeks in bottle.

DRY STOUT. Recipe for 5 gallons

6 lb. pale malt	11 oz. black malt
12 oz. crystal malt	1 lb. brown malt
1 pint wheat syrup	4 oz. challenger hops
Guinness yeast	Demerara, as syrup to S.G. 1.045°

Add crushed grains and wheat syrup to approximately 3 gallons of liquor and mash at 148° F, until starch end point. Strain off and sparge with liquor at 170°. Boil wort with hops for 40 minutes. Cool rapidly by adding balance of liquor. Adjust gravity with demerara syrup to 1.045°. Pitch yeast at 60° F, and ferment at this temperature. Bottle and prime. Serve after 6 to 8 weeks in bottle.

BARLEY WINE (hard water)

Definition. *With a starting gravity of 1.080–1.100° this will yield a heavy gravity beer of wine like quality. The closing residual gravity can be as high as 19°. Due to the high alcoholic* content there will be little or no head retention but there should be a lively and fast moving bead. The bouquet should be full and "fruity", and the taste smooth, round, and vinous. Barley wine should be kept for a considerable time to allow full maturity to develop.

Barley Wine. Recipe for 3 gallons

5 lb. pale malt	1 lb. crystal malt
1 oz. black malt	4 oz. wheat syrup
3 teaspoons gypsum	3½ oz. Whitbread golding hops
Demerara sugar to S.G. 1.083°	Guinness and champagne yeast blended, and latterly C.W.E. 67 general purpose yeast

Bring water to 154° F, add grist at 144–154° F, and mash to starch end point. Strain off, add gypsum and hops and boil for 40 minutes. Strain off. S.G. should be approximately 48°. Add sugar syrup to a gravity of 83°. When cool add blend of active Guinness and Champagne yeast. After skimming transfer to 1 gallon jars, fit airlocks and allow fermentation to proceed. When gravity is around the 20 mark the fermentation will show signs of stopping. At this stage pitch on C.W.E. 67 and ferment out. Bottle and prime in nips or ½ pints. Store for at *least* 12 months before serving. Ideal storage time is two years.

Lager (very soft water)

Definition. *This beer is produced in a completely different manner from the English system. The Decoction system is employed involving the use of various mashing temperatures. The liquor should be extremely soft, the malt is lighter roasted than pale malt. The hops are the seedless variety. The fermentation should be conducted at very low temperatures, that is 43–46° F, to allow the full flavour to develop. The colour should be straw, the bead should be very fast with a good head retention. The CO_2 content is greater than in English Bitters. The nose should be one of hops and grain, whilst the taste should be dry, full mouthed, and clean.*

Light Lager. Recipe for 5 gallons

7 lb. lager malt	5 oz. styrian golding hops
1 lb. flaked maize	Lager yeast
White cane sugar syrup to S.G. 1.040°	

Immerse grist and adjunct in 5 gallons liquor—COLD for 1 hour. Bring up temperature to 100° F, and hold for 30 minutes. Remove ⅓ of the wort and boil for 20 minutes and pour back on to rest of mash. Temperature now 130° F. Rest at this temperature for 15 minutes then again draw off ⅓ of the wort and boil for 20 minutes then return to wort. Temperature now 148° F. Rest at this temperature for 15 minutes and again draw off ⅓ and boil for 20 minutes and return to wort. Temperature now 160° F. Leave until temperature drops to 138° F. Restart heater to 145° F, until starch end point. Raise temperature to 165° F. After short rest draw off and sparge. Add hops and boil vigorously for 45 minutes. Cool rapidly and pitch active yeast. Conduct the fermentation in as low a temperature as can be attained—i.e. 43° F. Bottle and prime as normal. Store away in a very cool place for twelve weeks before serving.

Heavy Lager. Recipe for 5 gallons

8 lb. lager malt	White cane sugar syrup to
1½ lb. brumore	S.G. 1.055
1½ oz. crystal malt	Vierka lager yeast
	5 oz. Saaz hops

Mash grist and adjunct for 2 hours at 142–145° F, drop to 130–132° F, for 2 hours. Raise temperature to 150–153° F, until the conversion is complete. Boil wort with hops vigorously for 45 minutes. Adjust gravity to S.G. 1.055°. Cool rapidly and pitch yeast. Conduct ferment at 43° F. Bottle and prime. Store for 3 months.

Old Recipes
Birch Beer

1 oz. black birch bark	¼ oz. hops
½ pint water	½ oz. pimento
¾ pint golden syrup	½ oz. ginger
1¼ gallons water	Yeast

Make a liquid extract by boiling the ounce of birch bark in the ½ pint of water, straining and reducing liquor until it is as thick as treacle. Next boil hops, pimento, and ginger in ½ gallon of water for ¾ hour. Strain and stir into the birch extract. Boil up and stir in the golden syrup. Add remaining water and when cool add yeast. Bottle in the normal way and keep in a cool place.

Spruce Beer

To make spruce extract, if your are unable to buy it at the chemists, place into 2–3 pints of boiling water the young green shoots of spruce gathered in the spring. Boil until the water is brown and a strong flavour develops. Strain the liquor from the shoots, return to the pan, cover and boil until the volume is reduced by half or more. Bottle and store when cold.

Recipe for 1 gallon

1 lb sugar   1 gallon water
1 teaspoon spruce extract   Yeast

Dissolve sugar into the gallon of water and add spruce extract and when cool add yeast. Ferment and bottle in the usual manner. With this light starting gravity maturity will be quickly achieved.

Black Beer

This is a variation of spruce beer.

Recipe for 1 gallon

1 lb. black treacle   1 gallon water
1 teaspoon spruce extract   Yeast

Dissolve black treacle into the gallon of water and add spruce extract and when cool add yeast. Proceed as for spruce beer.

Mum

Recipe for 1 gallon

4 lb. wheat malt   ½ lb. oats
½ lb. ground beans
1 g. each of: cardus; benedictus; marjoram; betony; burnet; elderflower; thyme; pennyroyal
½ g. bayberries   Clarify with egg whites

Make and ferment as for ale. It is essential to keep this for two years. It produces a brandy type nose and taste.

Dr. John Harrison has researched many old recipes and the Durden Park Beer Club has made them. I append two here. Should you wish to research further his book of Old recipes can be obtained.

1850 Porter—1 gallon soft water

2½ lb. pale malt   7 oz. brown malt
1 oz. golding hops   2½ oz. black malt

Mash for 3 hours at 156° F, using 3 pints of soft water. Sparge with 1 pint of water. Remash grain for 1 hour at 175° F.

Sparge to make 1 gallon. Boil hops 1½–2 hours. Original gravity should be 60°. Ferment out with a Guinness yeast. Rack. Store in a one gallon jar.

1750 Original Entire Butt Beer

1 gallon soft water	3 lb. pale malt
½ lb. crystal malt	½ lb. brown malt
4 oz. black malt	2 oz. golding hops

Mash crushed grains for 3 hours at 156° F, as a stiff mash. Sparge. Remash for 1 hour at 175° F, and again sparge. Boil for 2 hours with hops. Strain and make up to 1 gallon at an original gravity of 80°. Ferment with a Guinness yeast. Rack and store in a 1 gallon jar.

Honey Beer. An Original Recipe

1 gallon water	20 oz. pale malt
4 oz. flaked maize	2 oz. crystal malt
C oz. golding hops	1 lb. honey, *not* **Australian**
Beer yeast	

Mash crushed grains in 6 pints of water until starch end point is reached. Put honey in remaining two pints of water and simmer, skimming off the impurities. Strain off wort and honey and boil with hops for 45 minutes. Cool rapidly after straining off. Bring up to full volume of 1 gallon, add yeast and ferment out. Bottle and prime as normal.

Hop Beer

1 gallon water	3 oz. cracked maize
¼ oz. bruised ginger	1½ lb. sugar
2 oz. fuggles hops	1 tablespoon malt extract
Yeast	

Put maize and malt extract into vessel and mash at 150° F, together with the bruised ginger. When clear strain off, add sugar and hops and boil for 30 minutes. Strain off and when cool add yeast, ferment out and bottle in the normal way. One may be tempted to raise one's eyebrows at some of these old recipes and their formulation, but try them and you may be pleasantly surprised, and it will be an experience to drink as your forefathers did all those many, many years ago.

CHAPTER XV

Judging Beers

Throughout Britain there are many major wine and beer shows and festivals, such as the National Association of Amateur Winemakers Conference, the Middlesex Festival, the Hertford, Wales and West of England, and Mid Southern Festivals. These organisations are primarily interested in the advancement of wine and beer making and therefore are a boon to the students of wine and beer. The amateur would do well to enter his beers into these shows where he would be assured of getting expert appraisal and constructive criticism The adjudication of all the entries is undertaken by members of the Amateur Winemakers National Guild of Judges. Since one can only gain entry into this Guild by taking and passing an examination, it follows that its members have a high degree of efficiency in undertaking the examination and judging of wines and beers. The Guild handbook, "The Judging of Home Made Wines and Beers" deals with every aspect of competitions and judging.

For competition purposes beer is judged under the following headings: Bottling Efficiency; Condition and Clarity; Bouquet; Taste Each section has a number of points allocated to it, totalling 30.

Let us assume for practical purposes that we are entering a bottle of beer in a competition. The first task is to make ourselves thoroughly conversant with the rules. Then comes the major task, that of preparing the entry. First: Bottling Efficiency and Presentation. Here we must ensure that we have a good, clean beer bottle. It can be brown, green, or plain glass. The method of sealing can be either a screw stopper or a crown cork. If a screw stopper is used it must be clean and unchipped and the rubber washer must be in good condition, i.e. very clean and in no way cracked or perished. The judge will look under the washer to see if there are any traces of dirt or old yeast lodged there. Chipped bottles or those with flaws will be heavily penalised and even disqualified, on safety grounds. Crown corks must be clean and free from rust. The bottle should be filled, allowing $\frac{1}{2}-\frac{3}{4}$ of an inch air space between the top of the beer and the bottom of the screw stopper or the bottom of the crown cork. The yeast sediment will be noted at this stage. Ideally it will be very slight. Further note will be made of any flocculence when the bottle is opened.

Condition and Clarity: Here the beer will be poured into a balloon type glass so that the glass is only partly filled. After the stopper or crown cork has been inspected the beer remaining in the bottle will be checked. It should be clean and star bright, with no signs of haze or yeast flocculence, in fact the yeast should remain fast. A lighted candle held behind the glass is of great help when performing this operation. After the bottle has been checked the beer in the glass is inspected. It should be star-bright, with a good head and head retention. A fine, lively bead should be observed. It is of the utmost importance that the atmospheric conditions should be taken into account. Beers are like some prima donnas, full of temperament and changing with the weather. If, for instance, the weather is cold the beer will be "starved". There will be little or no head retention, and there will be a loss of brilliance. When tasted the beer will be dull and somewhat insipid and lacking the crisp, clean taste of good conditioned beer. On hot days the beer will be "fussy" and "fret"; the head will be larger than normal and the bead will work at a frantic rate. Overprimed beers will even cascade froth out of the bottle, leaving little beer! On tasting, warm or hot beers will lack crispness and be cloying to the palate. The bouquet will be marred by the pronounced smell of the carbon dioxide gas. It is worth mentioning once more that the ideal temperature for beer is 58° F. Bouquet and taste will vary according to the type of beer being sampled, as we have seen in the chapter on Beer Types.

When testing beer ensure that the glasses used are kept very clean and completely dry. A trace of detergent, lipstick, or fatty foods will knock the head off any beer. I remember a person complaining about the flatness of the bitter he was trying. Since I was drinking the same beer and my bitter had an excellent head I could not help but ask him what he had had for his tea. Leaving out the unprintable parts, it transpired that he had enjoyed some boiled ham. I then asked him to wipe his lips thoroughly. I then bought him another of the same beer in a fresh glass. After due tasting the head on the beer remained perfect. When judging beer, therefore, the palate should be kept clean and fresh by swilling the mouth from time to time with water which is not loaded with chlorine or fluoride. An alternate is the Crispbread type of biscuit or the crust of a crisp, well-cooked roll. Avoid pappy, steam-baked bread, for it will only cloud the palate. Should you have a meal prior to judging avoid anything that is heavily flavoured or spiced, and, as the example has shown, avoid fatty, greasy substances. The use of perfumes, and heavily scented haircreams and oils is to be strongly deprecated. It naturally follows that no attempt should be made to adjudicate on beers in a room that has been cleaned with disinfectants, or some of the more heavily scented air fresheners. Admirable as it may be as regards hygiene, it is devastating to the nose.

Preparing your entries for a show should be done with meticulous care and attention to detail. The requirements already mentioned are not just a set of rules drawn up for the sake of competition, they are the outcome of long and careful deliberations designed to raising the efficiency and standard of all aspects of amateur brewing. They are meant to teach us the values of safety, hygiene, balance, and the true evaluation of the various kinds of beers we make. Since the inception of beer classes at the major shows the standard has risen rapidly. Dirty bottles, inefficient stoppers, heavy sediments, cloudy and flat beers are things of the past and have given way to products that are a joy to behold, surely a testimonial to the rules that are now generally adopted. The student should always remember that bad habits come easily and are hard to lose, whereas good habits take some cultivating, but once acquired one does not want to lose them.

There are several ways of preparing bottles which are to be entered into shows; here are two which have stood the test of time, and no doubt you will be able to evolve variations on these two themes.

First, the simple form. When the beer has been made and is ready for bottling sort out three bottles which are in good condition and free from chips and scratches. Check the stoppers for cleanliness and see that the rubber washers are in good condition. These proving satisfactory, get a clean siphon tube and prepare for filling. If the beer has been made correctly and the bottling time is right the beer at the very top of the container will be the clearest, so the siphon tube is inserted into the beer so that it is just submerged. The beer is *gently* siphoned into the bottle and filled to the required level, primed, and corked or screwed down. The same procedure is adopted for the other two bottles. They are then marked 1, 2, 3, respectively and set aside to mature. Number 1 bottle is the actual entry and Nos. 2 and 3 are the back-up or pilot bottles to be used to assess the value of the entry. After maturity is reached, and just prior to the show, the bottles are checked for lightness of sediment, after which one of the pilot bottles is opened and judged in the manner described. If it fulfils requirements, the No. 1 bottle is entered. The third bottle is a stand-by in case of emergency.

The second, and slightly more complicated method, is a form of degorgement as practised in the champagne industry. Here one siphons off the beer as in the previous method but fills the bottles to within a quarter of an inch of the base of the stopper. After screwing the stoppers down tightly the bottles are placed STOPPER DOWNWARDS so that the yeast can settle on the stopper. Give the bottles a slight rotary twist two or three times a day for four days. By this time there should be quite a build-up of sediment on the cork. Now is the time to remove this surplus, so get a bowl of clean water and fresh clean stoppers. Carefully carry a bottle, still neck downwards, and place the stopper under the water. Make sure that the clean stopper is at hand, unscrew the one in the bottle, letting it drop clear in the bowl. The slight build up of gas in the bottle will eject the sediment. Insert the little finger into the neck and wipe out any surplus sediment, and screw in the clean stopper. Repeat the operation with the other two bottles, then store away to mature in the normal way. This method is a little more intricate than the former but it is one which will bring good results after a little practise and the necessary dexterity has been acquired. A word of warning. Do not exceed the recommended four day period for the excess gas pressure build up could be dangerous. It is advisable to keep a check on the temperature during this period, remembering that 58° F, is the correct one to attain.

CHAPTER XVI

Cooking with Beer

Beer is not only beneficial as a beverage but comes into its own in cooking. Simple, effective, and tasty dishes can be attained with the use of beer. My wife Ruth until recent times lectured on cooking with wines and beers, and her talks on "Adventurous Cooking with Ruth Newsom" were highly popular. At home we enjoy our "Guinea Pig Parties" and I can recommend them! What, you may well ask, is a "Guinea Pig Party"? Well you sort out a four or five course meal, every course cooked with wine or beer. You select four victims (?) to sample the meal. What a pleasure it is to hear the "victims" calling for a slice of bread and see them mopping up that last drop of gravy! We supply menu cards which are old Christmas cards. On the inside left hand page we type the wines being served with each course, and on the right hand side we cover the "Love from your Aunt Fanny" bit with the food to be served. It adds to the occasion if such pleasantries as "Due to the shortage of serviettes a large shaggy dog will slowly walk round the table" are typed on the menu in bold print! In passing I am frequently asked what drink one serves with curry? So let us put this to rest once and for all: here is the answer. Cold lager, my friends, nothing more and nothing less. If you are planning a "Guinea Pig Party" why not try one of these recipes?

Soups

Brown soups can be improved by the addition of a wine-glass of strong ale or barley wine just before serving.

Beered Herring or Trout

Cook in mild beer. after which strain off some of the liquor and thicken to serve as sauce. A slight amount of vinegar can be added after the sauce liquor has been drawn off.

Casseroled Beef in Beer (A Ruth recommended recipe)

1 lb. stewing beef	½ pint of bitter beer
1 lb. small onions	1 beef stock cube
½ lb. carrots	¼ pint of boiling water
1 oz. plain flour	Salt and pepper
1 oz. lard	

Cut meat into cubes of about 1 inch. Scrape and slice carrots and skin the onions. Melt lard in a pan. Add onions and carrots and cook for 3 minutes. Add meat and cook for 2 minutes. Turn meat as it browns. Remove vegetables and meat, drain well. Leave fat in pan, stir in flour. Cook gently for 3 minutes or until browned. Stir in the beer. Dissolve beef stock cube in boiling water. Stir into pan. Season with salt and pepper. Put vegetables, meat and gravy into a two-pint casserole. Cover and cook in the centre of a pre-heated oven for 3 hours, or until the meat is tender. Oven setting, 300° F, or Mark 2. This recipe will serve four portions.

Stewed or Casseroled Beef

1½ lb. chuck steak	2 tablespoons dripping
2 onions	1 level tablespoon flour
1 clove garlic	½ pint brown ale
1 pint hot water	Bouquet garni
Salt and pepper	Pinch of grated nutmeg and
1 teaspoon vinegar	sugar
French mustard	2 slices of bread (¼″ thick)

Cut the meat into large squares. Slice the onions. Chop and crush the garlic with a little salt. Heat the dripping in a stew-pan and when it is smoking put in the meat to cover the bottom of the pan and brown quickly on both sides. Lower the heat slightly, add the onions and brown also. Dust with flour, pour on the ale and water, add the garlic, bouquet garni and season with the salt and pepper and vinegar and stir until boiling. Turn into a fireproof casserole, cover closely, and cook gently in the oven (340° F or Reg. 3) for 2½ to 3 hours. Remove the crust from the bread and cut each slice into four. Forty minutes before serving take out the bouquet, skim off any fat from the casserole, and spoon on to the bread. Spread thickly with the mustard and arrange on top of the casserole, pushing the bread down below the surface to make sure it is well soaked with the gravy. It will float again to the top. Put the casserole back into the oven uncovered for the rest of the time or until the bread forms a good brown crust.

Pork Stew with Beer

2 lb. boned stewing pork	¾ pint good lager
2 teaspoons salad oil	½ lb. finely chopped onions
¼ lb. thinly sliced carrots	2 cloves of chopped garlic
1 level teaspoon cornflower	1–2 level teaspoons salt
¼ level teaspoon pepper	5 tablespoons cold water
1 oz. butter	Chopped parsley for garnishing

Chop pork into cubes. Heat butter and oil in pan. Add onions carrots and garlic. Fry slowly, with lid on pan, for about ¼ of an hour or until vegetables begin to brown. Add pork cubes and fry more briskly until the meat is well sealed and golden all over. Add lager, salt and pepper. Bring to the boil, stirring. Lower the heat. Cover pan. Simmer for 1 to 1¼ hours or until the pork is tender. Add cornflower mixed to a smooth cream with water. Cook, stirring continuously until stew thickens. Simmer for 5 minutes, transfer to a serving dish and sprinkle with parsley. Serves 4 people.

Special Gooseberry Pie

Into a 1½ pint pie dish put 1 lb., of prepared gooseberries. Add 2 tablespoons of Demerara sugar. Add 6 fluid oz., of best bitter beer. Roll out short crust pastry and cover the top of the pie dish. Brush the top of the pastry with milk and sprinkle with a little sugar, not forgetting to make a vent to let out the steam. Cook at 425° F or Reg. 7 until gooseberries are tender and pastry golden brown.

Apple Fritters

Add to a pint of mild ale the yolks of 4 eggs, and 2 table-spoonfuls of sugar. Mix in a few cloves and a spoonful of mace, also a little salt and saffron. Stir thoroughly to make a good batter. Prepare the apple rings and leave them in the batter for roughly an hour before frying.

Welsh Rarebit

Using a double pan melt in a nob of butter and add 8 oz. grated Cheddar cheese. Add 1 tablespoon of mustard, salt to taste, also a little tabasco and paprika. Pour in a large wine-glass of bitter beer. When hot pour over toast and place under a grill to brown.

"Fromage a la Maison Irvin"

Take 4 oz. Cheddar cheese. Grate it finely. Add two or three chives (or to taste), finely chopped. To this add two tablespoons of bitter beer and work until a spread or paste is the result. Leave for 24–48 hours and serve with biscuit crackers.

Party Time

Heat thick slices of French roll in the oven and serve with butter with one or more of these cheeses.

British Cheeses

Wensleydale, Lancashire, Caerphilly, Cheshire, Stilton, Derby Blue Sage, Cheddar.

French Cheeses

Gruyere, Roquefort (made from sheeps milk), Brie, Neufchatel, Triple Creme (soft, ideally mixed with herbs such as fennel, rosemary, chives etc), Fondue de Savoie au Raisin (coated with grape pips), Camembert, Bleu des Causses (the blue mould has great diabetic value derived from the natural penicillium). For all these cheeses have mild pickles to accompany if required. Have a goodly selection of beers available.

The addition of barley wine, old ale, or stout to Christmas puddings and cakes greatly improves their taste and quality. Try making your pancakes using mild beer in lieu of a quarter of the liquid normally used.

INDEX

A

Audit ale 11
Anaemia 17
Ale wives 12
Allsopp 15
Alkalinity 26
Acidity 26
Acrospire 39, 42
Adjuncts 42, 43
Albuminoids 52, 54
Albumin varieties: 54, 65
   Albumin
   Fibrin or gluten
   Casein or legumin
Alcohol 59, 65
Alcoholic volume, finding
   the 69
Aeration, over- 73
Acetification 75
"Adventurous cooking with
   Ruth Newsom" 106
Aphis 37

B

Book of the dead 11
Boozah 11
Brewster sessions 12
Burton Abbey 13
Brewers company 13
Bass, William 15
Baverstock 15
Brewers show—exhibition 15
Bottles 19
Bottling 21
Bacchus 23
Burton Wells 25, 26
Burtonised water (formula 27
Brewing liquor 29
Boiled water 27
"Balling" 44, 62
Boiling 65
Barley wine 70
Barrel 74, 75
Barrel inspection 75
Barrel stink 75
Beer, sour 75
Bungs 75
Bottled beer 85
Bottled beer types 86, 87
Birch beer 90

Basic recipes 95, 96, 97, 98
   99, 100, 101
Bottling efficiency 102
Bouquet 102
Barley cake 11
Beans 44
"Budding", yeast 45
Beer engines 86

C

Cods wallop 12
Charles I and II, king 13
Campden tablet 19, 75
Crown corks and Crown
   corking machines 20
Carlsberg brewery 23, 45, 88
Carbohydrates 52, 59
Caramels 52
Cellulose 55
Cooling 65, 72
Calcium, organic and
   inorganic 66
"Cauliflower head" 73
Carbonated beer 77
Carbon dioxide gas 77
Carbon dioxide cartridge 79, 84
Colloids 81
Conditioning 92
Condition and clarity 102
Chipped bottles 102
Cooking with beer recipes
   106, 107, 108, 109
Couching 41
Champagne yeast 48
Casks 76
Cooper 77
Caragheen moss 96

D

Dutch 13
Doble—Doble 13
Decoction 14, 60, 63, 66
Dale, Arthur 15
Dairy quality plastic 19
Dextrin 55, 59, 60
Dextrose 55
Dickmaisch 63
Draught beer 75, 85
Diatomaceous silica 84
Draught beer types 86
Detergent 103

INDEX

Disposable bottles 19
Downy mildew 37

E

Etudes sur la Biere 23
Elements, of carbon, hydrogen oxygen, nitrogen 25, 54
Endosperm 39
Embryo 39
East Malling Research Station 33
Enzymes 45

F

Fahrenheit 15
Fermentation 20, 51, 72, 73
Fermentation control 72
Filtration 73, 81, 83
Firkin 75
Finings 76, 81
Finings, gelatine, casein, ox blood, white of egg, bentonite, agar agar, caragheen moss, isinglass 82
Filtration media, filter pulp jelly bag, filter cloths 83
"Fussy and fretting" beers 103
Flooring 41

G

Groll 11, 88
Gladstone 15
Guinness 15
Gambrinus 23
Gorbals water 26
German malster 28
Grain, wheat, oats, rye, maize barley 39
Germinating 40
Grain, break down 41
Glucose 53, 55
Gravity 68, 69
Glasses, balloon type 103
"Guinea pig party" 106
Grit 43
Grist size 44

H

History of beer 11
Highwaymen 13

Hansen, Emil Chris 15, 23, 45, 88
Harrison, James 16
Henius, Dr. Max 16
Hops 20, 30, 66, 88
Hops, curing 37
Hop varieties 30
Hops, wild 37
Hop, bracts or petals 31
Hops, seeded 32, 33
Hops, seedless 32, 33
Hops, triploid 37
Hopping, dry 76
Hops, testing quality 31
Hop concentrates 34
"Hopstabil" 34
Hop constituents 36
Hop, tolerant, resistant 37
Herodotus 23
Hydroxyl ions 27
Hydrogen ions 27
Honey 53
Hydrometer 67, 74
Hydrometer, capillary action 68
Hogshead 75
Haze 81
Honey beer 89
Herb beer 91

I

Infusion 14, 57, 60
Isis 23
Iodine test 61
Ion 27

J

Jacobsen, J. C. 16, 23, 45, 88
Jorgensen, Alfred 23
Judging beers 102

K

"Krausening" 74
Kilderkin or kiln 75
Keiselguhr 84
Kiln drying 41, 42, 43
Kaffir beer 43

L

Leeuwenhoek 14
Levesques 14
Lambert, L. 16

INDEX

Lauer 16
Lead glazed containers 19
Liquor, hard 24
Liquor, soft 88
Loch Katrine 26
Lupulin 30, 31
Lager 32
Lactose 53
Laevulose 55
Lauter tun 62
Lautermaisch 63

M

Moore, Mr. 16
Malt extract 20, 59, 69
Malting 39, 41, 43
Malt, lager pale, crystal, amber brown, black or patent 42
Milling 39, 44
Malt, quality recognition 43
Meyerhof 45
Maltose 55, 59, 60
Mashing 57, 72
Mash tun 57
Munich lager 85, 88
Mead 12
Mosaic 37
Modified malts 42
Mills, malts 44

N

Non return valve 80, 86
Newcastle brown ale 96
Non returnable bottles 19
Nutfield, Brewing Industry Research Foundation 33
Nettlehead 37

O

Osiris 23
Organic and inorganic solids, iron, chlorides, sulphates nitrates 25
Oxygen 66
Oxidation 73
Overpriming 103
Overfining 82, 84

P

Public house signs 12
Pilgrim fathers 14

Pasteur 14, 23, 45, 72
Pasteurisation 14
Peter the Great, Czar of Russia 16
Preparation 20
P.H. 26, 27
Pericarp 39
Palea 39
Phosphate, organic and inorganic 66
Pitching 73
Pin 75
Priming, re- 77
Pressure 77
Pressure gauges 77
Pilsen lager 11, 85
Preparing a bottle for show 104, 105
Preserving pan 19
Pumps 86

Q

Queen Elizabeth I 13

R

Requirements 19
Recipes: bitter, stout, lager brown ale 22
Rogue water 28
Rootlets 39
Rousing 57
Regulator valve 79, 86
Relief valve 79
Racking 92

S

Saccharometer 15
Schlitz, Joseph 16
Salt and glazed pottery 19
Sodium metabisulphite, stock solution 19, 75
Sugar 20, 52, 55, 69, 76
Sugar syrup 76
Siphoning 21
"Starter" bottle 22
Soft water or liqour 26, 27
"Steeping" 28, 41
Scutellum 39
Sorghum 43
Spaten brewery 45
Saccharomyces cerevisiae 45, 47

INDEX

Saccharomyces carlsbergensis 45, 88

Saccharomyces pastorianus I, II, III 47

Saccharomyces ellipsoideus I, II 47

Starch 55

Saccharose 55

Sparging 57, 61

Simmerstat 59

Skimming 73

Shives 75

Spiles 75, 76, 93

Serving tap 75

Spruce beer 90

Sickness in bottle 92

Star bright 18, 103

Specific gravity 68

T

Testing hop quality 31

Testa 39

Thermostat 59

Tannins 66

Temperature correction table 70

U

Urquell liquor 26

Unfermentable solids 70

V

Vacuum 33

Virus 37

Verticillium 37

Whitbread 16

Worthington 16

Water 25

Weihenstephan School of Brewing 35

Wort 60

Wort, filtered and unfiltered 72

Wye College 33

Y

Yeast 20, 45, 59

Yeast, high and low 45

Yeast, varieties 45, 47

Yeast production 47, 66

Yeast, spoilage, wild 47

Yeast, blending 47, 48

Yeast, slime forming 49

Yeast, autolysis 49

Yeast, disease ferments 49, 50

Yeast, purification of 50

Yeast sediment 103